I Am Why They Killed Diana

THE SECRET OF THE RED STRING...

Cynthia Queen of Scots
and America

ISBN 978-1-950818-60-0 (paperback)

Copyright © 2020 by Cynthia Queen of Scots and America

All rights reserved. No part of this publication may be reproduced, distributed, or transmitted in any form or by any means, including photocopying, recording, or other electronic or mechanical methods without the prior written permission of the publisher. For permission requests, solicit the publisher via the address below.

Rushmore Press LLC
1 888 733 9607
www.rushmorepress.com

Printed in the United States of America

Dedication

This work is dedicated to my twin flame, soul mate, my man, YUD CHET VAV. You are the key, I am the lock, Baby, I've been writing it all my life, inside me and it finally came out! You've said it best, "You ain't seen nothin' yet!" So you see my love, I've been paying attention, since that blessed day we played, in a MOTOWN swimming pool.

Forget You? Never! We need to be together again, to stop time and start FOREVERLAND, my friend. Golden Children, we are two, I'm your Baby, Love . . . MEM LAMED HEY, because you are the Sun, I am the Moon, while you are the word and I am the tune, playing. Love forever, The Lady, who is elegant, strong, honest and loving . . . Cynthia, Queen of Scots and America.

Preface

This work was written and self-printed in 2008. The Gunn's found America about one hundred years before Christopher Columbus.

    My direct Ancestor, Sir Knight Templar James Gunn High King of Scots and this new land America, was the first to step out of the boat, onto the land he and his crew found while out on a fishing expedition. Therefore, he became King of this land which is now called America. They came ashore in what is now called Massachusettes. King James died and is immortalized in Westford, Massachusettes. He likeness is carved on a cliff there and the year, of their arrival. Upon his death, his son Fergus Gunn, became High King of Scots and America. This was to be kept secret, until I'm writing to you today, December 16, 2019. There is a Monument and the carving there is called, the Westford Knight, with the year etched on that cliff. It is maintained by the Clan Gunn Society of America. Their cousin, Sir Knight Templar Henry Sinclair, was also a leader of the Expedition.

    Mary Queen of Scots, my direct ancestor was and is, until this very day, through myself, still has her blood coursing through my veins. Mary was true Queen of Scotland, Ireland, Wales and England.

    The secrets I have been trained by my Father William, the Last High King of Scots and America, are to be divulged in my books and then the last secrets, in public, when the time is just right.

    Mary's decreed via her instructions, that only one person knows the secrets and that is how, it has been passed down to me. One to one, my Father to me. I was trained to have them. We guard the the secrets with our life, ever since Mary died. Mary Queen of Scots was murdered, by Elizabeth the first, of England. King Henry and his harlot Ann Boleyn, were Elizabeth's parents. Elizabeth the second is a false Monarch, by rights I should be there in her place. Mary was and I, as her posterity, am the true Monarchs of all four Celtic Lands, not Elizabeth the second. Hence I am, the last Queen of Scots and America. Please enjoy the read. My Chapter One, starts on the page after my Black or White prose.

"Foreward,": To Benedict XVI, The Re-Declaration of Arbroath, in the Original, Latin . . .

Sanctissimo Patri in Christo ac Domino, domino Johanni, diuina prouidiencia Sacrosancte Romane et Vniuersalis Ecclesie Summo Pontifici, Filii Sui Humiles et deuoti Duncanus Comes de Fyf, Thomas Ranulphi Comes Morauie Dominus Mannie et Vallis Anandie, Patricius de Dumbar Comes Marchie, Malisius Comes de Stratheryne, Malcolmus Comes de Leuenax, Willelmus Comes de Ross, Magnus Comes Cathanie et Orkadie et Willelmus Comes Suthirlandie; Walterus Senescallus Scocie, Willelmus de Soules Buttelarius Scocie, Jacobus Dominus de Duglas, Rogerus de Moubray, Dauid Dominus de Brechyn, Dauid de Graham, Ingeramus de Vmfrauille, Johannes de Menetethe Custos Comitatus de Menetethe, Alexander Fraser, Gilbertus de Haya Constabularius Scocie, Robertus de Keth Marescallus Scocie, Henricus de Sancto Claro, Johannes de Graham, Dauid de Lindesay, Willelmus Olifaunt, Patricius de Graham, Johannes de Fentoun, Willelmus de Abirnithy, Dauid de Wemys, Willelmus de Montefixo, Fergusius de Ardrossane, Eustachius de Maxwell, Willelmus de Ramesay, Willelmus de Montealto, Alanus de Morauia, Douenaldus Cambell, Johannes Cambrun, Reginaldus le chen, Alexander de Setoun, Andreas de Lescelyne, et Alexander de Stratoun, Ceterique Barones et Liberetenenetes ac tota Communitas Regni Scocie, omnimodam Reuerenciam filialem cum deuotis Pedum osculis beatorum.

Scimus, Sanctissime Pater et Domine, et ex antiquorum gestis et libris Colligimus quod inter Ceteras naciones egregias nostra scilicet Scottorum nacio multis preconijs fuerit insignita, que de Maiori Schithia per Mare tirenium et Columpnas Herculis transiens et in Hispania inter ferocissimas gentes per multa temporum curricula Residens a nullis quantumcumque barbaricis poterat allicubi gentibus subiugari. Indeque veniens post mille et ducentos annos a transitu populi israelitici per mare rubrum sibi sedes in Occidente quas nunc optinet, expulsis primo Britonibus et Pictis omnino deletis, licet per Norwagienses, Dacos et Anglicos sepius inpugnata fuerit, multis cum victorijs et Laboribus quamplurimis adquisuit, ipsaque ab omni seruitute liberas, vt Priscorum testantur Historie, semper tenuit. In quorum Regno Centum et Tredescim Reges de ipsorum Regali prosapia, nullo alienigena interueniente, Regnauerunt.

Quorum Nobilitates et Merita, licet ex aliis non clarerent, satis patenter effulgent ex eo quod Rex Regum et dominancium dominus Jhesus Christus post passionem suam et Resurreccionem ipsos in vltimis terre finibus constitutos quasi primos ad suam fidem sanctissimam conuocauit. Nec eos per quemlibet in dicta fide confirmari voluit set per suum primum apostolum vocacione quamuis ordine secundum vel tercium, sanctum Andream mitissimum beati Petri Germanum, quem semper ipsis preesse voluit vt Patronum.

Hec autem Sanctissimi Patres et Predecessores vestri sollicita mente pensantes ipsum Regnum et populum vt beati Petri germani peculium multis fauoribus et priuilegijs quamplurimis Munierunt, Ita quippe quod gens nostra sub ipsorum proteccione hactenus libera deguit et quieta donec ille Princeps Magnificus Rex Anglorum Edwardus, pater istius qui nunc est, Regnum nostrum acephalum populumque nullius mali aut doli nec bellis aut insultibus tunc assuetum sub amici et confederati specie inimicabiliter infestauit. Cuius iniurias, Cedes, violencias, predaciones, incendia, prelatorum incarceraciones, Monasteriorum combustiones, Religiosorum spoliaciones et occisiones alia quoque enormia et innumera que in dicto populo exercuit, nulli parcens etati aut sexui, Religioni aut ordini, nullus scriberet nec ad plenum intelligeret nisi quem experiencia informaret.

A quibus Malis innumeris, ipso Juuante qui post uulnera medetur et sanat, liberati sumus per strenuissimum Principem, Regem et Dominum nostrum, Dominum Robertum, qui pro populo et hereditate suis de manibus Inimicorum liberandis quasi alter Machabeus aut Josue labores et tedia, inedias et pericula, leto sustinuit animo. Quem eciam diuina disposicio et iuxta leges et Consuetudines nostra, quas vsque ad mortem sustinere volumus, Juris successio et debitus nostrorum omnium Consensus et Assensus nostrum fecerunt Principem atque Regem, cui tanquam illi per quem salus in populo nostro facta est pro nostra libertate tuenda tam Jure quam meritis tenemur et volumus in omnibus adherere.

Quem si ab inceptis desisteret, regi Anglorum aut Anglicis nos aut Regnum nostrum volens subicere, tanquam inimicum nostrum et sui nostrique Juris subuersorem statim expellere niteremur et alium Regem nostrum qui ad defensionem nostram sufficeret faceremus. Quia quamdiu Centum ex nobis viui remanserint, nuncquam Anglorum dominio aliquatenus volumus subiugari. Non enim propter gloriam, diuicias aut honores pugnamus set propter libertatem solummodo quam Nemo bonus nisi simul cum vita amittit. Hinc est, Reuerende Pater et Domine,

Quod sanctitatem vestram omni precum instancia genuflexis cordibus exoramus quatinus sincero corde Menteque pia recensentes quod apud eum cuius vices in terris geritis cum non sit Pondus nec distinccio Judei et greci,

Scoti aut Anglici, tribulaciones et angustias nobis et Ecclesie dei illatas ab Anglicis paternis occulis intuentes, Regem Anglorum, cui sufficere debet quod possidet cum olim Anglia septem aut pluribus solebat sufficere Regibus, Monere et exhortari dignemini vt nos scotos, in exili degentes Scocia vltra quam habitacia non est nichilque nisi nostrum Cupientes, in pace dimittat. Cui pro nostra procuranda quiete quicquid possumus, ad statum nostrum Respectu habito, facere volumus cum effectu.

Vestra enim interest, sancte Pater, hoc facere qui paganorum feritatem, Christianorum culpis exigentibus, in Christianos seuientem aspicitis et Christianorum terminos arctari indies, quantumque vestre sanctitatis memorie derogat si (quod absit) Ecclesia in aliqua sui parte vestris temporibus patiatur eclipsim aut Scandalum, vos videritis. Excitet igitur Christianos Principes qui non causam vt causam ponentes se fingunt in subsidium terre sancte propter guerras quas habent cum proximis ire non posse. Cuius inpedimenti Causa est verior quod in Minoribus proximis debellandis vtilitas proprior et resistencia debilior estimantur. Set quam leto corde dictus dominus Rex noster et Nos si Rex Anglorum nos is pace dimitteret illus iremus qui nichil ignorat satis novit. Quod Christi vicario totique Christianitati ostendimus et testamur.

Quibus si sanctitas vestra Anglorum relatibus nimis credula fidem sinceram non adhibeat aut ipsis in nostram confusionem fauere non desinat, corporum excidia, animarum exicia, et cetera que sequentur incomoda que ipsi in nobis et Nos in ipsis fecerimus vobis ab altissimo credimus inputanda.

Ex quo sumus et erimus in hiis que tenemur tanquam obediencie filii vobis tanquam ipsius vicario parati in omnibus complacere, ipsique tanquam Summo Regi et Judici causam nostram tuendam committimus, Cogitatium nostrum Jactantes in ipso sperantesque firmiter quod in nobis virtutem faciet et ad nichilum rediget hostes nostros.

Sanctitatem ac sanitatem vestram conseruet altissimus Ecclesie sue sancte per tempora diuturna.

Datum apud Monasterium de Abirbrothoc in Scocis Sexto die mensis Aprilis Anno gracie Millesimo Trescentesimo vicesimo Anno vero Regni Regis nostri supradicti Quinto decimo.

Endorsed: Littere directe ad dominum Supremum Pontificem per communitatem Scocie.

    Names inscribed on some of the seal tags: Alexander de Lambertoun, Edwardus de Keth, Johannes de Inchmertyn, Thomas de Meiners, Johannes Duraunt, Thomas de Morham (and one illegible), and Cynthia Anne Marie Gunn, Queen of Scots and America, who herself, Re-Dedicated, 6/6/2008.
    SCRIPTI, SCRIPTI, FINI.

Amore,
Cynthia

HIStory

In silhouette you gaze past blinds, their handheld flames are burning. Liberty's likeness you bring to them, you're there the music's curling. Spotlight in view, my God it's You, behold you lights flare in view.

On Automaton arm to stretch you from yon, the Thames to Lausanne, Barcelona and the Champs elesee, et al Köln, to London anon, where upon you return, no crosses they burn. Oh, how I yearn! Airplanes return, your landing my concern.

Throngs gather.. alas your face! You're here, the world embrace, they can't believe it's really You! Now waving, at babes, dog tag on blue. Must duck and cover, round cars they hover. To see your hand they'll hours stand.

Corral the sheep, who mourn and weep a flowers grasp and you are humbled. Photo op moments, with Mickey, you never grumbled. Geisha girls and boys arranged in Pyramid, their bated breaths, for you to be amid. Your script on their trust, they run to touch your hand, a finger, hoping you'll linger.

You did your part, my twin flame, soul mate, now let me do mine. The color red, the proper attire, your warrior dress regalia, they desire.

Passing bobbies, backed by troops, you're ready now, flowing, glowing, gleaming, the voice, the melodies, the moves, the messages, all from You . . . streaming.

The explosions around you, the water pouring forth from your body, they all need to be near you, to hear you, to see you, to feel you, to see what is real You . . .

Oh my love, how you slay me . . . Oh, you beautiful man, the apple of my eye, of course I'll tell them why. They're crying and fainting, the light shines through you, a sea of souls, reaching, hoping, feeling, knowing, that you my beloved, are THE ONE. You're healing. With Liberty's stance, you propel upwards a yard off the floor, the cameras capture the launching. They see you at shore.

The Knight Templar wields his sword to the fiery face of the Dragon, destroying it in a blaze of glory, no rhyme. You emerge with the angels all around you. They're waving for Moon Walking, your love talking.

Soon, you appear from the light, the wind is blowing my love, the white sheets unfurling, they stop . . . they stare, they faint, they're flowing, over seas of arms, they wail and moan, they see the truth, away they go to healers, to see you they're feelers . . . still you continue on.

They bear the name on their foreheads, they're screaming in ecstasy's reigns, as in beds. You make your stand and wave your hand, the lights are white and glaring, there . . . they've seen the light, you take your stance, my God, my Love, they're praying!

Your hat goes on, they wear then you in awestruck wonder, they're crying to see you yonder. In the round you're dancing, they're flying, testifying, jumping, whirling, kneeling, you strike the pose, revealing. "Walking on the Moon . . . my feeling . . ."

Five beautiful boys on golden cover, ABC the number three, you look at me, like when we played together as children, so precious in your hat and fly cord coat, smiling, near the tree, the portrait in gold, I'm across the sea . . . the moat.

You tip your hat you're on your toes, time stands still, the lights expose, music with bows, going places, with other faces, the five come shining through in view. Switch to live, it's still the five, I see the eye, the cosmic swirl, a hurricane unfurled. The destiny at waters edge, like pearls. The distant lightning strikes on ledge, the eye again that sees . . . below the arrows tip, alas, WE know, the Pyramid is rising.

Look at you . . . you're OFF THE WALL . . . the mirrored sky is calling them all! You're beautiful, you reappear, this time it's me you're calling, we're falling. ROCK WITH YOU, the night away . . . we're hauling. Don't stop my love, crown is blazing, you strike the pose, cosmos explodes, now you're grazing, gazing, softly lying, amazing, the colors bold are raising, and yet . . . loves hold.

To "THRILL HER," now you're trying, she's flying, no denying. Your face appears, then danger nears, an outstretched leg is whining. Rock with you? Look, there's Paul, white gook and clowns, amid the crying. It's dangerous and then you howl, with golden eyes and teeth, like Cowal, entwining. The claws come out and too the horns as spikes, the dead right now are staring.

They're reaching up to catch your lead, the blood-red suit you're wearing. Shining, you pulse, the toes, you're up again, black, white, amid their pining. You point and look, smiling in the Pharaoh's nook, spinning gold dust, amid spear points thrust; you're BAD in patent shining.

Street toughs gather at your command, you open their door to gently command, to gently hand, a snip, a sprite, dancing in the night, out on the street, snap, then dance, embrace that beat. Pose, the cover shows, full measure of your prose, you sing on toes, the plate then switches, stare down those witches, the ultimate question, in the looking glass fishes.

You're on the run, from crime that's done, smooth as the silk now running, with the pit bull, over golden loft concrete mountain tops. Looking out you see the night, ELECTRIC EYES in everywhere. You beam bright glow, from the depths of Nod, whoa! Until the face explodes, mouth with water, teeth gnashing, you step in time, too DANGEROUS with bones, Elephant man, ball and chain, to which they all will carry again.

You're first amid the Carnival, now above them all you're standing, blue light point down to toes, on tip of boots, with buckles dangling. Another taste of you, my love, you're wrangling, shaking hands with no glove, the touch, the pulse, your body's grinding. Dance and sing, give the look and point, then strike the poses, shades, no shades, up again, on toeses, you're MOSES, the hall of VANITY'S FAME FAIR climbing.

Relaxed, you look out, to find me rhyming. Your crest in view, defining. Me aligning, OBE ONE CANOBE . . . tour last you say it so be? The black storm soon arising, the Reich book bears your face true love . . . Oh, wait! Paris is chiding, them chiming, to you on book HITKRANT . . . what's this!!! Another country . . . calling? . . . Elephant?

In every language of the earth, yourself they are revering Gleaming white and glove shades, on skin, now look . . . you're peering. Skiing, climbing, pepper the salt of the Sergeants flock, with flavor still remaining . . . The eyes of us . . . the ones who know, the truth, my Elephant star, we're sailing.

The peacocks reign now DANGEROUS, the King and Queen we're raising, no flailing. BUBBLES and Angels, upon the wings, will give us flight from "SOUREGNAD'S," things. Earth's upside down, they've done it now, your watchful eyes are gazing. Again, through time, you pierce their veils, to see their wretched crumbling, climbing . . . whales . . . the monster machinery, of their fathers due dinosaurs, escape on ladder gleaning, stairway to Heaven? . . . We're careening.

The warning again . . . the look, the window, blue ball shatters the silica sand panes, you're back my love, your eyes are trailing, like trains. Kick the orb blue, Jordan's friend at court, it's you who runs through the carpal tunnel . . . hotel in view. You rip your clothes, awash in blue, hue lights, shining like morning dew.

You take your stance and yet again, our romance, whilst blue angels you emit. Winging . . . whirling, winding, above the pit.

You've done your part, we're one true heart, our worlds collide, I do abide and you decide. Alas . . . to make the fix on BLANKETS, I will be bringing. I am young inside, so reach out for me, I'm clinging. Come hither my love, I'm singing, no song sung blue . . . so BRACE YOURSELF . . . REMEMBER THE TIME, my dove, we're from above, it's TRUE . . . we're still in love, forever your Golden Ewe, sharing THAT BEAT called love . . .

Cynthia

Black or White

Above the clouds you fly toward me, the Moon, I see you coming. You pause, trek down a city below, I focus on streets, you're floating. A house ahead, you turn . . . it's their approach, while parents fading, toward boy in room, air guitar in hand, giraffe and posters waiting, jumping, happily thumping, on floor, on ceiling too, now revealing, no feeling.

The pitch, the hit, he's ticked a bit, then sees four bobble heads nodding, equalizer throbbing. He's on the bed, jump, snap, kneel, Pop's face turns red, no sobbing instead . . . he's creaming, a boy gleaming, happily, playfully, teaming. Now up the stairs, Pop puts on airs, to teach the boy a lesson. Door opens, the lads chagrin, shown on the chin, to see the mad complaining. "What's wrong? It's fun never to hurt anyone?" Yet still, the Dad remaining . . . Lad pleads his case, yet still the face, the mean who hate song sailing. The threat . . . he's scared . . . door slams . . . breaks tears . . . ICON PICTURE, unfailing

Yes, Oh Yes! The shards fly loose, upon a floor, oh no . . . the image tumbles. He's crushed at first . . . the raise . . . the brow . . . the thinking . . . now . . . Unsnap the guitar case, huge speaker in room, slid like a BROOM, to JUMP in place, then poses with SCOOPER, UFOSES, Listen to MOSES, the truth coming.

Input, alignment, small space confinement, yet once the plug is lifted, into guitar, on red light afar, hearing not impaired, the dial turning far past the peg to, "ARE YOU NUTS?" Shades on the face, black glove in place, affixed. Oh . . . now she's looking . . . just long enough to see, he's tough, wipes mouth in rough, then stares to what is coming.

"EAT THIS!" he roars, and feeds their fears, the window panes exploding. Blue light, Dad's flight, into the night, through rooftop, he's raising . . . there where afore the Moon, who waits . . . come soon . . . Blue glowing, Indigoing, where's he going? The not knowing is showing.

Scene change to dusty mountain ridge, the down upon the grasses, lays the lioness and child of jungle's king, his tail contently wagging. "All's well," he roars, "we're safe, of course," from rampant tribesmen hunting she hears, he nods, who creeps nearby? . . . It's spears, to try and kill her Lion. They're creeping . . . still . . .

Chair lands, until he's stopped on Serengeti, to see you jump among the tribe; my God, you are proclaiming, "Let's do this dance, across the plain," to which I see my love, you're clapping. Now run to set, to girls who get, straight up in oriental fashion, the whirl, they kick, with you they stick, while through their fingers they . . . switch to me, little girl Cherokee, alas my love . . . we're dancing. The tribe all around us, to protect romancing, the HORSEMAN ride, we never break stride, you point the Sun is shining. You take my hand, my joy command, what's this . . . so now we're reading?

People are bleeding? She's right there with you, smokestacks in plain view, they drive machines to NOWHERE, we dance and whirl, I'm your girl, we have shown, we are not alone. Then, the snowflake angels flow . . . into Cossacks, dipping and spinning around you, you're winning, the message shows true and clear, you're in the round, they're bowing down, My God, in line now prancing, spinning, bowing, it's fine you're winning.

Blue orb with snow, you're winning, they're all inside, trying to hide, from my reach beginning I pick them up, our Toy, come into view, we both babes on planet sitting. You black, me white, it's day and night, at once, we two are playing. Just us, alone . . . upon the orb, made just for two hearts beating. That's what this gold smoke, when you reappear, now as a man, inflaming. The hell I wrought on us . . . can you forgive? My love . . . I killed, burned cross, it was myself and not the one called Caining.

You reappear to set me straight, I need your firm rebuking. For down through time, I did the crime of Abel's death by nuking. I built machines, at serpents' behest, to kill those who came after; for I alone, brought tears to earth . . . it should have been just laughter..

Forgive me . . . forgive me, now switch to street, our children ghetto hanging, thank God you're there, he's got blonde hair . . . with shades now I am panging. He points to me, you all stand firm, you guide them past the money, gold Cadillac chain, red slapping five feet, dancing, you watch, they're telling. He circles face with bling on hand, you stand beside him kindly, they all look sad, that I was BAD, to bring them up so blindly. Yet now I see, around the torch, you come to see me Honey . . . I take the blame, killed Liberty, my shame, you point, you move, I'm in the groove, I love to see you happy! Moving in time, ahead of this rhyme, you waited for me I'm coming, Big Ben, Eiffel, come into view, yet still your lamp light burning.

Across the sea, you came to me, like the torches we still carry . . . Oh Ancient of the old, Sphinx Temple I behold, and wait for you . . . to marry. Forever in love, we their faces now above, I see them morph through Babel, the Tower I built, to try and hide, that Cain did not kill Abel.

The time for truth, I give to youth, of every land and nation. I'll right my wrong, my love, I'm strong . . . I have the information. Hollywood, set to go, Black Panther, is in motion my love; you see . . . that God told me . . . they'll fall into the ocean.

Past Templar, Washington, you leave, the zone, now out on street, then staircase you strode on down to change around, erect now standing then place the hat upon your head, in Bo Jangles spotlight landing. You look at me, come face to face, I know what I have done, keep well my love, I have great news . . . the battles I have won!

You start to move, the pause and stance, to make sure I am looking . . . feet in the round, you're on the ground . . . Alas you're waiting. I jump out of the garbage can, the Leo cat noise making you turn, to look, I've caught your eye, blue haze to street, you go to prove your meaning.

Peel back, top shirt, expose winds truth, you're still, there's no betweening Wind stops, you stand, now right in direction, pointing you move with grace. Find the pool of water, that's been standing.

You kick your heels . . . splash, from the pain you've suffered, then make the signs across yourself.

You start toward the sidewalk, wet shoe you lift. They made you dance, to imitate Gene Kelley; I see it now, the inner pain deep inside your belly. You kicked their bottle, then throw the hat, to give what they've got coming . . . Detroit, their ills, which broke men's wills, with cars, you now are smashing. Crowbar lashing, they deserve the thrashing!

Triumphantly, you show them signs again of just what is coming, with hands on self . . . you reach for me . . . I'm waiting with intense yearning. Give me your seeds, I'm here . . . agreed? So throw their wheel for turning. Break down the door, you are the key, I am your lock, I'm waiting.

Show them again, we're one, it's done, and when you leap from metal, you grab the can to throw at sand glass door . . . the wind is blowing. Blue smoke through veils, of peaceful bliss, you start to feel my body, I'm here my dear, so come, draw near. Royal Arms Hotel for two? . . . Me and You, spinning in my water, you release a son, a daughter; so take me now, my love, I'm waiting. We'll wear no clothes and then expose, our loves to all the HATERS . . . You've won! They're done! Broken down by Gunn! Now 'round you blue angels reigning. Old Royals . . . will pass! You broke the glass, they're done, you did the slaying! They tumble down and fall on ground, you overcame their CANCER. They did their deeds but now they're done, move over . . . here comes the PANTHER!

So sit tight, my darlin', take pause on rub, whilst let ME entertain YOU . . . from ABOVE.

Love, Cynthia.

Chapter 1

Diana died, so that I could live. Are you ready? Let's go! It's time to get real. We all know about the Pharaoh and Moses, we all know about Christ Jesus, right now.

I'm going to explain how we got into this mess and how we can get out of it, so PLEASE, just sit down and relax, pay attention, reserve your questions for later . . . and, I will tell you what happened and how we can correct it. If we don't do it now, the doomsday clock is set at thirty seconds to midnight and before we destroy ourselves and burn up the planet, we only have this one LAST CHANCE to usher in the thousand years of PEACE promised!

Lamed Vav Vav. Hello, this is Cynthia. You knew me before I was in my Mother's womb. What do I remember? Do I really have to do a review? Okay, I will. At ten months I walked, at eleven I ran and I've been running ever since, in every sense of the word.

What have I learned? Okay, I'll tell you. Who were my parents? William Thomas Gunn, Senior and Celene Anne Pilecki. Who was William? He was born in Decatur, Alabama, son of Joseph Rike Gunn and Ruth Lewis Gunn, she, a direct descendant of cousin Meriwether Lewis, of the Lewis and Clark Expedition. Joseph was the son, of Big Daddy Gunn, who carried the secret, down through time and taught it only to my father, William Gunn.

It is an ancient Celtic name, of Scotland and before which, I will reveal the origin of the name; and the secret it holds for our time. Suffice to say, the family credo, "Either Peace or War," will be part of the secret, I have been instructed, by my Father William, at the proper time and place, the secret time, of the ultimate decision.

For now, more about William . . . William was born on the cotton plantation of Joseph's father, Big Daddy Gunn, who also had oil in Texas. The Gunns were successful, because they were kind. They treated their black workers, as workers, even during the slavery; their workers were precious to them because they'd be nowhere . . . without them! The workers lived in good houses behind the mansion and not in shacks, at the back of the property

My father, William, had a black nanny. His father, Joseph, was a huge disappointment to Big Daddy. He took up his life, as a professional riverboat gambler, brothel owner and an alcoholic. That hurt Big Daddy. So Big Daddy knew that Joseph was not the one, to carry the secret.

When the Great Depression came, it took everything. Big Daddy died. Joseph would only come home to visit a couple of times a year, from his escapades. Where was home, now? William, his mother Ruth Lewis Gunn, and my father's sister Betty, had to live and work on another man's plantation, at the back of the field and they lived in the shacks, with the former black slaves, of another owner, a non-family member.

So you see . . . my father came into the world in riches and at a very tender age, I think before seven, his life became a to rags story. William did the best he could, to help his mother Ruth. This went on and on for years, until William graduated Decatur High School in 1947.

He worked in a flower shop down town, making wedding and funeral flower arrangements Every day, he dreamed about making life better. How? Every day, he passed the Navy recruiter office, near the flower shop. One afternoon, the voice . . . the, "word of knowledge," inspired him to walk in.

The recruiter decided, because of William's intelligence, he needed an appointment to Annapolis. The Senator was contacted and he was placed on first alternate. A few weeks later, he got a telegram, requesting his presence at an interview with an Admiral, Rickover, in Washington.

That day came. Sitting in the waiting room, with a dozen other men, a young female navy lieutenant called them one by one, into Rickover's office, in alphabetical order. William noticed that the men were coming out red-faced and disturbed, by the yelling and slamming noises, coming from the Admiral's office. Now, it was his turn!

The lieutenant said, "Mr. Gunn, the Admiral will see you now!" They walked in, there was a long metal conference table, abutted to Rickover's desk, with three chairs on either side and one chair at the door. "Take a seat Gunn!" barked the Admiral. My father said, "Which seat Admiral?" "This seat Sir," said the lieutenant.

"Goddammit Lieutenant! I told you never to address anyone beneath you as Sir! Now get the hell out of my office, before I ship your ass off to Alaska!"

Well, Dad went to the first of three seats, on the left side. Rickover leaned back, hands behind head, feet on the desk, he screamed, "Closer Gunn!" as Dad's butt nearly touched the chair. Dad moved to the second seat . . . butt nearly again on chair, "I said, Closer Gunn!" Rickover screeched.

Dad took the first chair, slammed it on the side of Rickover's desk, plopped his butt down and screamed, "Is this close enough Admiral?!?" Rickover, said nothing . . . sat up in his chair, folded his hands on the desk, and said, "Gunn, I like you! now . . . you can have your damned appointment to Annapolis, with all those fancy boys . . . OR, you can come with me, on the greatest adventure of a lifetime and I'm going to give you thirty seconds to answer, Gunn," looking at his watch, "and now you only have twenty five seconds . . . what's it gonna be Gunn?"

To which Dad instantly retorted, "I want to come with you, Admiral." And so began Dad's naval career, he went to Arco, Idaho and was hand picked by Rickover, to be his personal assistant, in the navy, on loan, to the Atomic Energy Commission, Rickovers eyes and ears and even surrogate son, for the next twenty three years.

Who was Celene? Celene, my Mum, was born in Norwich, CT., daughter of Stashia Cwiklinski and Stanley Pilecki, first-born generation; polish Americans through Ellis Island immigrant parents. Celene was raised as a Polish-American Princess and Dad would call her that.

Celene was beautiful, intelligent, kind, loving, giving, a thespian who loved the Arts . . . all the Arts. She was an unassuming waif of a girl, when she met Dad a strapping, handsome, intelligent genius, bound for greatness in his career.

When the met, it was ELECTRIC! For four long years, they courted until they could wait to marry, no longer. And so, they did and welcomed William Junior, into the world in 1954.

One hot summer's day, in July of 1959, the 28th to be exact . . . I was born. Dad was in Arco, Idaho, away for the Admiral, as usual, my Godfather, Joseph, Mums cousin, took Dad's place at the Subase Hospital. He was there always . . . for me and Mum.

When did I know I was here? Well at 22 months. It was a warm, Camden, New Jersey May Day, of 1961.

I remember climbing out of my crib, putting my Stride-Rites on the wrong feet, walking past Mum, asleep on the couch and pushed my way, through the loose back screened door. I sat on the hot cement stoop and then decided to walk the fenced-in yard. I walked the entire perimeter; I crept around the garage, which had an 18 inch wide strip of lawn to the left. I sat there for a while, soaking up the warm sun.

The next thing I knew, I heard Mum screaming, "Cindy, Oh My God! Where are you?!? Please God, please, I beg of you, I love you, where are you, Cindy?

I listened . . . after an eternity of her chanting and crying, over and over, the same prayer . . . she appeared at the far edge of the gap. "Thank you God! Thank You! Come here my baby . . . I've found you . . . Oh My God! Thank you!" I slowly went into her arms.

Who was God?!? Who had helped my Mummy? How could I know, that this episode, would be the beginning, of my journey . . . on the sea of consciousness? . . .

Cynthia

Chapter 2

So the question becomes again? When did you first know you were here? Well, it was on that day, on the side of the garage. I knew I was here . . . when I saw myself in my Mother's eyes. She was so grateful, to God, that she had found me, from that day forward, I visually studied people. All, people.

The first few years, were pretty uneventful . . . Soon, it was the summer of 1963, on one hot August day, we broke down on the Jersey Turnpike. Mum, Nanna Stashia, Billy and I. No one stopped at the hour mark

Mum began to cry, Nanna comforted her, it didn't work. When I noticed this, I began to pray, I stood up, leaned on the back seat back, folded my little hands and said, "Dear God, please send someone to help Mummy." Thirty seconds later, a highway patrol officer arrived. I remember it well. Mum and Nanna marveled saying to one another, "She IS the GOLDEN CHILD! God listens to her . . . she has BLIND FAITH!"

Soon, it was November, Mum and I went to the seven-eleven, to get bread and milk. Inside, all the adults were crying, this scared me, they told us . . . "President Kennedy was dead in Dallas." The next three days, were spent glued to the TV.

On that first night, Dad indicated his plans to attend with Rickover. We all thought it was a good idea, for him to do that. We stayed home Mum and Billy and I, even though we had an opportunity to go. We stayed home and we watched it and that is when I first saw television.

What is television? And what did I see on it? Well, I saw people, masses of people, for the first time. I studied what they were doing, on the box inside our house, which they came in through.

What were they doing? Walking, by a long box, in a building, with a flag draped over it, and men dressed like Dad . . . were standing nearby. I remember looking intently, Mum said to watch it and to look for Daddy and the Admiral, but . . . I didn't see them. But, I did see Jackie, Caroline and Jon-Jon and all the others. I studied all of it. Mum explained it to me, including President Kennedy, being dead and in the box and that the Lady, was the Mummy, and the little ones, were their children. I cried, that their daddy had died . . . and then the horse . . . the rider less horse . . . all the way to Arlington and the cemetery and the lighting of the eternal flame.

I came away from that experience hungry, to observe everyone, everywhere, from that day to this. Come with me, on the journey of a lifetime . . . I promise, when you're done reading this or listening to this, you will get it. Soon after the Kennedy incident, I studied my next media experience, radio.

I memorized "Ferry cross the Mersey," by Gerry and the Pacemakers. Mum and Dad had me sing and perform it for them. It wasn't much longer and I began dancing, they used to have me dance and sing, along with water color painting, coloring and sticker fun. The next item to tackle was time.

The clock was introduced when Dad, brought home our Dachshund, Peanuts. She was a beautiful animal and I played with her constantly. One day, puppies arrived, six puppies. Mum would tell me what time something would happen and I would watch the clock, until it did happen. Mostly, I waited for Dad to come home, so we could play together. Dad was hands-on all the way. I would watch the hole in the house, the front door, for him to appear. The clock and the door told me when.

Mum was all about cuddling, kissing, loving and the arts. Celene, Serene Celene, as she was later in life to be known, was my sunshine. She would sing, "Only Sunshine and Eyes for You," every day and night, as she lulled me to sleep. We sang it to each other, in unison. A high soprano, professionally trained in Norwich, Connecticut, by a woman who was paid, to travel specifically to give her lessons, from New York City.

Mum, was also the great thespian. She was the lead player in many productions, in Norwich Free Academy and at the Masonic Temple, in town. This woman loved life, loved us and loved others, despite her alcoholism.

What is alcoholism? It is debilitating, a drug addiction, alcohol is the oral liquid remedy to a persons problems, or so they think and feel, when they drink it. When did you see your Mum drinking alcohol?

Well, I remember that day as if it were yesterday, as all my memories, are like yesterday. I was sitting on the kitchen counter, at four years old, with Mum holding me and giving me my Vydaylin, the liquid children's vitamin. I always would get a double dose, because I asked for more. This day, as I was put down, Mum reached into another cupboard and drank out of a different brown bottle. I remember the recoil, the shake of her head and the sound, "Haw!" I said, "Haw Mummy?" She broke down and cried, sorry I had finally seen her addiction, at such a tender age . . .

Cynthia.

Chapter 3

Very soon after the, "Haw," incident, the SHIT hit the fan. One night, in the wee hours of the morning, I heard it. What did you hear? My worst nightmare, this first night of terror, hell and damnation . . . hit me like a ton of bricks. What was the ton of bricks?

Well, I woke up to Mum, screaming and crying, to the sound of a beating and glass being smashed, all over the house, begging and pleading, "Please Bill, don't do this . . . I'm sorry Bill!" I opened my bedroom door and stepped on glass. I didn't know what it was, I only knew my feet were in agonizing pain and bleeding. I continued to walk in the glass, down the hall and saw the scariest sight a child should ever have to behold.

What did you see? I saw Mummy on the floor, being beaten and kicked by Daddy and he continued to break everything in sight to my horror, he soon went to the attic, trap door, outside my bedroom. He was throwing glass bottles, with alcohol in them, into the hallway. I ran to my Mother . . . and comforted her and protected her, for I knew of his beatings . . . first hand, for discipline, that's how Billy and I were beaten, whenever he thought we needed it. That was his true form of discipline but now, he was doing it, to Mum!?!

In my four year old mind, I had wondered what she had done bad, to be beaten? When Dad was away at sea or stateside for Rickover, the house was peaceful. I honestly began to look forward to the breaks. What were the breaks?

They were the times I didn't have to go to bed, every night, crying and begging. "God . . . Dear God . . . please don't let Daddy beat Mummy tonight, please . . . I beg of you, I love you, Goodnight." This became my night prayer, faithfully, each and every night, whenever he was home. It was good, that the Navy and the

Atomic Energy Commission job, with Rickover, required him to be away almost six months of every year.

When he was home and each weekend, thereof, was a cocktail party, at either our house or another officer's house. Billy and I had a host of babysitters, in our lives, it became the norm.

In the daytime, I would go to launchings of ships, air craft carriers and submarines. The Navy social ladder . . . ah . . . is very steep . . . and steeped in alcohol. What do you mean steeped?

I mean all the adults, got smashed drunk, at those cocktail parties and balls. The house parties were casual dress, so I never knew the men's ranks. On the nights of the balls, Mum, beautiful, would wear her latest creation, a dress she had hand made and on the sewing machine.

Soon, I was sewing, myself, straight seams and helping fold simple laundry, as my chores. What are chores? Aha, chores are the tasks given to us by our parents, to earn an allowance. The allowance is money given for the chores, money earned. I was taught the value of a dollar, on the side of the road, at my first business, at four years old, I sold lemonade, rather, Dad sold the lemonade, while I played.

What is playing? It is the place where we lose all of our cares and inhibitions . . . a time when we are joyful and full of imagination. The imagination is the seed of wonderment and possibilities, a place and frame of mind, to escape to and so . . . I escaped.

Being the child of a military officer, I learned at a very tender age, to make friends, wherever we lived, or I was going to be a very lonely person, young girl. What is lonely? Well . . . it's the state of mind, or time, when no one else is with you, in person, or in mind . . . or in absentia, one can be in a room, full of people and yet, feel all alone and helpless.

What is helpless? It's the feeling you get, the sinking feeling, that makes you feel all is lost, all is not well and things, will never get better. The beatings became bizarre to me, I reasoned at four, that Mummy couldn't help drinking alcohol, she needed it . . . somehow? Just as a child needs to experiment, with how far we can go, before we get into trouble.

We push the envelope; we test and decide all situations and people, all day, every day, that's what we do. I reasoned, she was being punished, like we children. I just couldn't figure out how these grown-ups, all of them, including Dad, could drink the alcohol, at our house parties or those away or the balls, and only my Mummy, was getting beaten!?! Like a bad child, a bad girl, for doing it?

Cynthia.

Chapter 4

That fall of 1963 was a very busy and unusual time, in more ways than I've already described. It was in that fall, of '63, that I first went to school. What is school? Oh yes, school, it was three days a week, that I was to go to school. It all started on a warm September day, balmy like summer. Mum took me to a large brick building, down the street, from my first awareness of moving, for the Navy, in Newport News, Virginia. As it turns out, I was born at the Subase, New London-Groton, Connecticut, lived in Pascagoula, Mississippi, then Camden, New Jersey, prior to Virginia.

Now, the sight of this Hilton Baptist Day School made me aware, that I had been moving around. I would attend this school, about three days a week. The main thing that sparked my awareness, of my surroundings, that very first morning . . . Dad had given me a huge lecture, to be a good girl, listen to the teacher and above all, be careful, be aware of your surroundings, a message he would resonate, throughout my life.

It was important to him and Mum and anyone charged with my care, that I be safe. A contradiction, even hypocrisy, because he himself, made me feel unsafe, during the beatings, no matter if it was me, Billy or Mum, who was receiving them. The first day of Hilton Baptist Day School, I remember Mummy crying through the chain link fence, as I walked hand in hand, with the teacher. The nearer I got to the brick school, Hilton Building, the further away and smaller she got. That was the day; she could no longer keep me close at hand. It was time for me to learn and socialize at school.

What occurs at school? Well, it's the place that we go to learn, grow and socialize with our peers, children our own age and some younger or older. The pre-K Kindergarten Day School, which I was attending, was fun! I took finger-painting to a new level! I began, to help the teacher with the other kids, from day one, when they would fall asleep.

I would sit with the teacher and sip white milk out of the carton and get to know her. I was ready at four, to see adults as they are . . . people, just larger versions of our self. I began to study the teacher and the kids in my surroundings, I would hug and kiss my classmates, when they would fall or they got hurt and got sad or just cried. I made sure; they were on their pallets, for naptime and loved to watch them sleeping peacefully.

I did not nap. I was, and am a constant observer, Kennedy did that to me. What is an observer? It is one who watches, listens, does not judge, only sees and hears things and understands, if those things are right or wrong. What is right and wrong? Well, it's the difference between good and bad. Good behavior brings happiness, bad behavior brings despair. Despair, is a sister to hopelessness, joy, on the other hand, is a sister to bliss. I will speak more on bliss later . . .

Of course, from that time, until it was time to move to Scotland, I entered the Pre-K, Kindergarten and then first grade. Despite the beatings, I lived happiness from the inside of myself. In January of '66, we were re-stationed. I remember Dad, saying to Mum, that Rickover said, "Okay Gunn, it's time to do your overseas duty, where do you want to go?" To which Dad said, "I'm Scottish, how about Holy Loch, Scotland?

The next two months, were spent in preparation, to go to Scotland. During this time, we got our shots, for overseas duty. The shots were brutal, we had several, the worst of which was typhoid, you have no idea how this shot, slams a person. It slammed me, Mum and Billy and for the next several days, we were like zombies, the walking dead. I remember feeling intense pain, as if I had been beaten by Dad and then slammed up against a wall, with broken aching bones and the horrible high fever . . . this went on for several days, it made me hate shots, hate needles and fear the needles, forever.

Once we recovered from the shots, it was time to learn how to write my name in cursive, longhand, at six years old, I was made to, write over and over, Cynthia A. Gunn. I hated the times Dad would make me write it all night, when I came home from school.

In February, I was sick, or sick again . . . this time I would spend twenty four hours a day, several days, on the couch in the living room, on a rubber sheet, covered with cotton sheets. Over and over, all those days, Mum gave me alcohol baths, to try and break my high fever. It could not be broken, it continued to rise and as I gasped for breath, sweating, I was in entire body pain and crying. When I could take it no longer, I prayed, "Dear God, please help me!"

Instantly, I was out of my body, flying down a long, long, crystal hallway, belly down, as Superman flies, the Light . . . ah . . . I was flying toward the Light and it was brighter than our Sun. Its colors twinkled, on the crystal walls of the hallway and I was soaring, toward that Light! The closer I got, the more I slowed down . . . I heard a voice say, "She has to go back."

Instantly, I was back in my sick, tired body. Mummy picked me up and rushed me to a nearby civilian hospital, where they fed me penicillin. I remember her rebuking and scolding Dad, for only taking me to navy doctors saying, "She almost died!"

In a few days, I was better, then stronger. We had a big day, when it was time to get our identification or, as they say, ID cards and passports, pictures black and white. Now, that signature, I had struggled with, was put to the test! Daddy was so proud I did it!

With passports in hand, we went home to greet the movers. Who are movers? They pack and ship everything we could take overseas. The rest went into storage. Unfortunately, Peanuts could not go with us, quarantine would be required and Dad couldn't put the dog through it. I was devastated, my first big disappointment, my dog was taken from me.

Cynthia.

Chapter 5

The day came for us to leave, for Decatur, Alabama. It was our last visit stateside, we were visiting Gran, Dad's Mum and his sister Aunt Betty and my cousins, Nancy Jo, Virginia and Laine. We had them, us, two Dachshunds, Peanuts and Teeny Weeny, her puppy, in the car. We were on the Huntsville, Alabama, side of the river.

I was sitting directly behind Dad, who was driving. I noticed the flatbed truck, with no load, was coming closer to the car, I screamed, "Daddy, that truck is going to hit us!" He swerved, as the truck made contact and we landed on a single short piling, a telephone-like pole, cut at about three feet above the ground. We stopped. The car began to smoke, from under the hood; the car was teeter-tottering on the post, with the deep river below. Dad and I remained calm. The others . . . panicked!

He, *assessed* the angle and decided, everyone needed to exit, through the right hand side of the car. The whole time I prayed, "Dear God, please don't let us fall in the river." As Dad and I exited the car, he scooped me up and said, "Good Girl! I'm proud of you, Honey!"

We spent an extra two weeks stateside, waiting for the huge repairs to be made to the car. All was well . . . *except* for one awful night . . .

We were at Gran and Betty's house. I was playing dress-up in costumes of dance, with the girls. Betty came home drunk and then it began . . . the beating.

He beat her mercilessly over and over, saying, "You're a good for nothin' drunk!" Just as he had been doing, the same thing to Mum, all the while, all those years, I had seen him doing the same thing, to

Mum and now, he was doing it to Betty! I couldn't believe that no one would help her, as I helped my Mum, at every beating.

They were all afraid of him, I was not. I've never been afraid; I don't know what it feels like. Instead, I just did as I had done in Mums case, tried to stop him from pummeling Betty and as usual, I took a beating, to try and stop him. Billy, on the other hand, five years my senior, did what he always did, hid. At home, it was in his room, there, it was on his cot. Mum was sober and got to see, what he did to Betty.

I watched her, watch, in horror, too afraid to intervene, I did and paid dearly! Finally, the car was ready, so we drove to JFK Airport, for the Pan Am flight, across the pond, to Bonnie Scotland. We flew at night, in a heat lightening storm, in early April.

I remember boarding the plane and the stewardesses, pinning a wings pin, on me. Billy slept, I did not. After what seemed like an eternity, up in the airplane, the green patchwork quilt fields, with stone walls . . . appeared. We were in Prestwick, Scotland. Soon we were in Dunoon, after being driven by an officer.

We checked into a bed and breakfast, in the town. It was run by the MacLarens. These people were over sixty. We stayed about a month, during which time we bonded to them. They became like Grandparents to us. Mrs. MacLaren, didn't live much past when we moved, to the luxury apartment, we waited for at "Onich," Toward by Dunoon, at the Frasier Mansion, on the Firth of Clyde.

When we went in to pay our respects, she was laid-out, in the living room, in the same parlor; we had spent so many fun days and nights, with her.

What does laid-out mean? That is when a person is placed in the open, long box, the casket. The casket . . . is the same box, I first saw on TV, at President Kennedy's lying-in-state. With, the flag draped. Now, it was time, to learn and see, face to face, in that living room, why people were put inside, when they died.

Mum and Dad did the best they could, to explain her death. They told me she had been very sick, but that it ended and that she went to heaven. I did not question it, I remembered touching her cold lifeless hand, when I knew she must have went, to the same place that I did, before I was back in my very sick body, just months before when I had suffered the bi-lateral Pneumonitis.

People came and went, crying and mourning. I was in no position, to tell them where she went, because, we were taught by Dad, "Children should be seen and not heard." I was beginning to understand when to speak and when to quietly observe. The manners and etiquette of a naval officer's child . . . were my cloak.

The next day, brought the funeral at St. Mun's, in downtown Dunoon. This was familiar territory, as I was a student there. I was placed in the second grade, for about two weeks, upon arrival, to the school.

Soon, I was elevated to the forth grade, because Scottish curriculum, was about fifty years, behind American, at that time. Now, I was with children two years older, yet struggling to learn the text. Again, I became the mini-teacher. My peers, on the playground, played with me yet . . . kept me at arms length. The nuns placed me in charge of the milk count, for the entire school.

Each morning, I would pass to each class and take the head count, silently, for the day. It wasn't long, before I knew every student, in each grade and took the attendance, to the superior's office.

Cynthia.

Chapter 6

One early spring day, I was called to the Mother Superior's office. I thought I had done something wrong. Instead, I was told . . . I needed to go back to the second grade class, for catechism I was required, only to prepare me, for my Roman Catholic First Holy Communion. I had remembered my church experiences, until that time and saw all those, who went up, out of the seats, but never, knew why.

What is first Holy Communion? . . . the time when children, first make a first confession, or penance, in preparation for the communion. The nuns explained the fact, that we needed to be cleansed of all the bad inside, our deeds we'd done, just before going into the church, to receive the body of Jesus Christ.

We needed to hear, "Body of Christ!" from the priest and then reverently say, "Amen." Meaning, "I believe!" and take Christ's body on our tongue, no chewing, just let Him melt on your tongues . . . they would tell us . . . and He would be Living, inside of us, the nuns told us . . . Intently.

They also instructed us, that now; we were of the age of reason, the knowledge of good and evil. The date for Communion, was set in May and Mum and I, began our quest for my Communion dress and veil. We took a day, to go to Glasgow. The ferry, took us across the Firth of Clyde and a train from there.

We left early in the morning and had an incredible day. We searched, until the right dress, ah yes . . . veil and shoes were purchased. It was so much fun, going on a special day, for a special outfit . . . then that grand day came . . .

I was so excited . . . that the Jesus, I had prayed to, would suddenly be inside of me! I only knew He was . . . Jesus . . . my friend in Heaven . . . at that tender age. I knew where He was, because I had almost gotten there, on my journey, to Heaven, months earlier, in the crystal hallway.

Even though I began to know Him, as He entered my life, my body, I continued to pray directly to God, Always. The seriousness of Roman Catholic Religion enveloped me. I got it! I began to expect that all other people, starting with Mum, Dad and Billy, should get it too! I remembered, there had been an Uncle, in the United States, Father Walter, whom I would see in the summers, back at Misquamicut Beach, in Rhode Island, at his cottage and also at the Pilecki homestead, in Norwich, Connecticut, the farm homestead.

I understood now, that he was a Priest first and therefore, an Uncle . . . second. I was intrigued, that I had an Uncle a Priest. I recalled the summers, back in the States, at his and my Aunt Mary's cottage, as I mentioned to you a moment ago. Mum, Billy and I summered there, every year, when Billy got out of school or when I got out of school. The summers of '66 and '67, we did not go back to the States. We stayed in Bonnie Scotland.

Shortly, after first Holy Communion, the most horrific beating occurred. It was a huge party night at "Onich," our home. All the usual officers and their wives attended, all the adults, again, just as through the years, became falling down drunk. I thought all would be quiet, no beating, for Dad was drunk too. That was NOT the case!

Dad found a letter; Mum wrote but never sent, to her tour guide, from her recent European trip. It made him insanely jealous. He flew through the house, intermittently beating her, breaking everything in sight and spilling out, all the alcohol bottles, in the kitchen, where the floor, was about one inch below the dining room, the result was an alcohol pond in the kitchen. He beat Mum unconscious for the very first time.

I got Billy out of his room; I made him come out . . . because I thought she was dead. When Billy tried to revive her, Dad beat him mercilessly, stripped her naked and told him, "You Love Her! You Love Your Mother! So Much . . . Have Her!" as he made him simulate intercourse, on her passed-out body . . . and said over and over, "She's your Mother . . . have her . . . have her . . . we're not enough for her anymore!" And then, beat Billy . . . mercilessly!

In a while, then, Dad went back into their bedroom . . . and locked the door . . . even Dad at that point, retreated, of his own self imposed disgust!

Billy and I said nothing! . . . to each other, as we sopped all the alcohol, in towels and wrung them out, at the tub, into the night. We got Mum, bloodied, torn night gown and bruised, into my bed. I slept in the chair outside my door, as she wept and Dad ranted in their room.

The next morning, I had Mum get in the tub and I helped her to bathe. Her face was disfigured, with eyes, nearly swollen shut and huge black eyes and a bloody, swollen nose . . . just terrible! . . . lips, huge and split. She spent the next two weeks in sunglasses day and night.

Dad stayed on the ship, Simon Lake, for several nights, until he cooled down enough, to return. And he did! As he had always done . . . no remorse, no I'm sorry, no I'll never beat you again . . . He just pretended nothing had ever happened. Mum and Billy, pretended it too.

I, on the other hand, never pretended it didn't happen . . . or never would again . . . I knew it would and in the fullness of time, it always did. When December of '66 came, I went into the garage one day, to get my bike. I saw a beautiful new pram, baby doll carriage, in the far corner. I said nothing . . . about seeing it.

When Christmas Day came, the pram was under the tree. I was told Santa had brought it. Of course, I knew . . . when I laid eyes on it, that there was no Santa. I told no one. I rededicated myself to vigilance . . . to the study of adults and to seeing things realistically. I was aware; there were no fairy tales that were ever true.

What is a fairy tale? Ah yes, those crafty stories we're told as children, to get us to pay attention and affect our behavior, or set unrealistic goals for us. I started to see people and life at face value. I learned every action, has an equal and opposite reaction. I dreaded New Years Eve and all of the cocktail parties, Mum and Dad attended.

Each brought a beating, for Mum and terror, for us kids.

Cynthia.

Chapter 7

The decision to tour Great Britain and the continent of Europe, was made early in 1967. We had been living in the Frasier mansion, "Onich," Toward by Dunoon and enjoying its lovely grounds and its situation on the Firth of Clyde. Father and Mother, decided it was time for us to prepare, for the journey, our pilgrimage to the Vatican, which needed to be done.

In April, we had a practice camping trip, on Loch Lomond. The days and nights in the April Scottish climate, took much getting used to, yet, it was necessary, to prepare us, for the twenty five days to come, camping in Europe. One fine, Scottish morn, the four of us decided to go fishing, in our rented row boat, on Loch Lomond.

Our camp was at waters edge and the boat tied to a tree, whose roots extended into the Loch. After about two hours of children and Father, William, fishing, Mother, Celene, announced, "Bill, I don't think there are any fish in this lake!" At the very second she uttered those words; I felt the jolt and heavy sinking feeling, at the end of my hook. "Oh! My God! I think I just got one!" I shouted gleefully, trying to manage not letting the fish, strip the pole from my hands.

Dad guided me through the entire process, of playing the fish, until it was tired, which took about fifteen minutes, of me reeling in, letting out line and over and over, the same procedure, until I could finally crank the reel and see the fish at boat side. It was the most exciting, exhilarating, experience of my childhood, until that day. I named him, "Sammy, Salmon," and . . . the three of them let me! Even though, they knew he was a pike! That day, Dad carefully wrapped Sammy, in a towel and took him to the nearby village fishmonger. When he returned, he said, "Sammy is worth thirteen shillings, Sweetie! What do you want to do? Sell him? You need to decide, because it was you, who caught him." I could not at that moment.

I snacked on a strawberry apple tart pie, Dad bought for all of us, in the village and pondered.

After a short while, I told him, I wasn't sure yet, what I wanted to do with Sammy. He set Sammy up on a stringer, tied to the same tree in the water, as the boat. I'd take walks around the camp, then to see Sammy tethered to the tree, by metal loops, through his mouth and gills. It hurt me to see him that way, yet every now and then, Dad reminded me, "thirteen shillings!"

That night, was a long sad one, with me praying to, "Dear God, what shall I do about Sammy? I don't care about the money, he looks so sad on that chain!" I cried silently and wiped tears, until soon, I fell asleep. In my dream, his Mummy was crying, through the water for him, "Sammy, Sammy, come home Sammy!" Upon arising, I knew what I had to do. I announced at camp breakfast, which Dad had made, that, "I'm letting Sammy go . . . I don't care about any thirteen shillings, I love him, I don't want the fishmonger to kill him, it's not fair, his Mummy wants him back!" "Okay," Dad said.

Soon after, we released Sammy. It was time to break camp to head home to "Onich." Along the way, we stopped at, "Rest and be Thankful," just as we had always done, on our weekend car trips, around the Scottish countryside and highlands.

The late June time came and we swam the cold waters, of the Firth of Clyde, in preparation for the cold waters to come, in Europe. Dad said we needed to condition ourselves, that this is why, we camped, fished, swam and did all the outdoor living we could, after all, "We are the Gunns!" he'd tell us.

We drove down to London, for a few days stay. We took in all the sights, which all tourists do, the palaces, the tower bridge, the royal ships, Big Ben, Westminster Abbey, downtown London and of course, Piccadilly Circus. There were many things now, which I reflect on, which no other tourists were near us, through the entire London and Europe trip, which strike me now, as being necessary, because of who I am. I will speak more on that later. For now, let's just say, that access to things others do not see, or are not seen doing, were normal for our family, on this pilgrimage.

The exact order, which we visited all the countries we did, is mostly clear to me still, suffice to say, we did go to those places necessary. Dining outside, became the norm for us. We'd eat breakfast and dinner at the campsites and take lunches out, each day, mainly at sidewalk cafes and many times, sitting at tables with complete strangers, as Europeans do, to share available seating space and break bread, with other people, from all over the world. My eyes were first opened, on the Pan Am flight, across the pond, but our weekend car trips and this pilgrimage, simply put the extent of life and space on this planet and the different peoples, who live in different countries, different ways, into view. It was all becoming clearer to me, then crystal clear, that we were not alone in America, in fact, we were the, "new country on the block!"

As I took in, all the ancient sights and cultures enveloping me, I made a pact with myself, never to forget a moment, be aware of my surroundings and as Dad would say, "Kids, the world is your oyster, soak it in like a sponge!" All the while, camping, for two or three days, at different destinations, in . . . France, Belgium, Holland, Germany, Switzerland, Italy . . . Wow! Superb! How exciting!

And so, I did just that. The first impressions were of London and all her splendor, grandiose and historical as it is and with Dads history lessons, in each location, we visited, in each country, it was there, that I saw my first rude awakening, of mans inhumanity to man.

We had taken a double-decker bus downtown, to Piccadilly Circus. We were going out sightseeing, all day. We had just finished dinner, outside at a restaurant and stepped out to the pavement. Now on that sidewalk, we stopped to hail a cabbie, back to the campground. We walked past a huge toy shop, with a huge teddy bear, which filled the front window. I asked Dad to buy it for me.

He said, that he could not, because we had just begun our trip and, "What would we do with it?" I said, "Tie it onto the top of the car!" Well, of course, that was not possible . . . I started to whimper as we walked along and then saw a most shocking sight! . . . a wretched, dirty, unkempt, seemingly totally drunk man, on the sidewalk, lying in a corner, next to a door jam, with flies, all around him.

His clothes were old and filthy and he smelled, awfully bad. I stopped to see if he was alright and he pulled his topcoat away, exposing himself, stroking his penis and ejaculating, on the spot! My father and Mother scooped me up, I said, "What's wrong with that man?" They played the whole incident down, saying, "He's sick, he's poor and no one loves him, so what he did, was because he is so sad. Pray for him Cindy, he needs your prayers!" And so, I did and the incident passed us by.

London was so regal, to say the least. Westminster Abbey, with its artifacts . . . Oh! . . . made a huge, impression on me. We toured the city, truly extensively. Try though I might, I could not get the royal guard, to flinch, at Buckingham Palace. I tried all my best attention getters, but to no avail, they didn't even seem to breathe!

The next run was to, the White Cliffs of Dover and the ferry, to Calais, France. Those cliffs are as white as snow and it is awesome; to watch them, get smaller and smaller, on the ferry crossing. France was beautiful, but a brief car trip, that first day we landed there.

Belgium and Holland were beautiful, with their ships in canals, windmills and endless fields of flowers, there, were two brief stops, in those countries. Next it was on to Germany, Italy, Switzerland, where we'd spent the lions share, of our vacation pilgrimage. Dad was right, to have us conditioned for camping and swimming, in the icy cold waters.

Most nights and mornings, were chilly sweater weather and playing in the icy cold waters, especially the great Rhine River, of Germany and beautiful Lake Lugano, in the Swiss Alps. All through the journey, I was taken to all the great cathedrals, of Europe, the gothic, majestic *Köln* Cathedral in Germany, stands mightily beside the Rhine, with its two spires, pointing to the heavens. We went to all the usual tourist stops. I remember putting coins, into the snow white and seven dwarfs fountain and immersing my right hand, deep into its waters.

To see the great botanical gardens by cable car and visit the *Köln* Zoo were awesome! I had the opportunity to see my second Giraffe and all the other species, up close, as we had done at the London Zoo. Mother and Father, one fine German morn, announced, "Today will be a long one kids, so prepare yourselves we're off, to tour the castles of the Rhine. I didn't mind the hard work and the fast pace of it all . . . we were used to packing up, breaking camp, moving and setting up camp again. We were very nomadic, as our Viking and Scottish heritage, was ingrained in us. Mum, although a Polish-American Princess was a good sport and supported her three Scots, all the way. God bless her heart . . . even with very severe asthma, she was our good trooper.

Cynthia.

Chapter 8

The Rhine River cruise, started with a ferry ride, on the Lorelei, up river, from port Mainz. The cruise was slow and peaceful, with an excellent tour guide, pointing out all the historical places and castles, along the shores. We had moved, to a camp nearby, Rudensheim on the Rhine, for this leg of our journey. I had seen many castles in Scotland and England and now I was to be treated, to the sight of even more.

I remember, my first favorite of sights, on the cruise, was the famous Mouse Tower, along the beautiful scenery and serenity of the hills and the river, where Castle Ehrenfels Ruines, Frankenburg, Bad Salzig at Boppard, Die Pfalz, Kateberg, Ruine Nollich at Lorch, Die Lorelei, Spay Villages at Niederspay, Marksburg at Braubach, Castle Ehrenfels, Castle Stoltzenfels and then, of course, the beautiful town of Koblenz.

The return trip, from Koblenz to Mainz was on a train, which moved much faster, back to our port of call and yet, still afforded us the opportunity, to see the sights, once again, by rail. How exhilarating! We were all, exhausted that night and decided, to eat at a campground snack bar. We dined on picnic tables, on bratwurst and pom fritz, as we call them in America, French fries. Dad announced, from today forward, it's going to be just as busy . . . so be prepared . . . tomorrow we are going to Lake Chimsee, to Herrin Island, we must see King Ludwig's Dream Castle . . . Dream Castle!?! I wondered . . . all night, just what could it be?

The boat ride to the castle was great fun, but then again, I was used to boat rides to various Navy ships, submarines, destroyers, ship tenders and of course, the grandiose, majestic, air craft carriers.

From where the castle boat docked, it was down the pea stoned way, to the castle, which was the width of the castle itself. The closer we got, a beautiful fountain, came into view. There were tourists, outside on the grounds, yet . . . when we arrived, we were asked to wait, until they could clear, the inside of the castle, for our private viewing.

This was the first time of many, we would be asked to wait . . . until a site could be cleared, just for our family's private, personal visit. I remember walking, just the four of us, up the opulent staircase, on the entrance balcony. Inside the castle, our private tour and guide, left no stone unturned. We spent about two hours, just our family and a tour guide, viewing, how another country's royal family, once lived. We were given the option to dine, in King Ludwig's private hall of mirrors. Dad declined, saying instead, that we needed to keep moving . . . to afford the tourists, to come back in.

My favorite spot, inside the castle, was the bedroom of King Ludwig, I pretended that it was my own and dreamed of waking up there, one day, to the roaring fire, which I could envision, as I gazed at King Ludwig's, bedroom fireplace, which was made from a single, solid, piece of porcelain and adorned with gothic symbols, solid gold and a huge white cherub, in the middle of the mantle.

It was in that bedroom, that I first heard from my Father, "Someday, I will explain just who you are, Sweetie, but for now, you are my Scottish- American Princess . . ."

When the castle tour was over and we stepped outside, was the first time that I noticed, that the tourists were grumbling and commenting, "Who are they . . . that they had to wait so long . . . for them to finish their tour." Dad told me to ignore their displeasure and just pray for them, because they were probably jealous."

No Big deal . . . I let it go . . . and that evening, we were treated to dinner, at a beautiful German Restaurant, adjacent to the Lake, of the Castle, at Chimsee.

I couldn't believe the courses that came out, one right after another, at about 9:00 p.m., a dance troop of men, in traditional leather shorts, with suspenders and German accent clothing, complete with hats . . . and the ladies, in their colorful, full skirted, multi-colored German dresses, with braided hair and bonnets, appeared.

For an hour and a half, they danced, to a full German band, of their ethnic dances, spinning, whirling, stomping, locking arms, sashaying and the men, slapping their legs and arms at various intervals I was enthralled! Yes, I had been a highland dancer, back in Scotland, but this! . . . This was magical. I never wanted it to stop and it kept going . . . until, they were exhausted.

Soon, a bouquet of roses was presented, to Mother. The artists greeted us and we congratulated them and marveled at their expertise. They were so humble, thanking us . . . for coming to see them. All through the night in my dreams, I saw them, I wanted to repeat that day, the next day, but Dad said, we were a bit behind, in our scheduled appearances, so we needed to make up time.

At breakfast, the next morning, Dad told me, "You need to wear your dress today, because it will be easier, being a salt miner!" We drove to Saltzbergwerk . . . Berchtesgaden and were whisked into various costume rooms. Mum and I, to Ladies and Girls . . . Dad and Billy, to Men and Boys. When we met again, outside the fitting rooms, the guides asked if we wouldn't mind, riding the train, below, with the tourists? Dad said, "Of course, we won't mind!"

We were told to wait, until they had the train loaded, with four spots, for the four of us, at the engine. I remember all the tourists looking at us, as we walked past them, to our reserved seats at train's front . . . and so, the trains ride to salt mines below, began.

When we got off the train, at the point below, there were a series of rock hewn halls, cut into the underground and a series of one hundred foot or more long slides . . . or shooty-shoots as the yanks called them.

Wooden slides, which propelled in darkness, to lower and even lower levels, until finally, the salt in the earth . . . appeared

We were issued small pick axes, to tap our own souvenirs, which were placed in boxes, according to type. What fun! Hundreds, maybe even a thousand or more feet, below the earth's surface. I must admit, a rickety, wet elevator, propelled us back to the station at the topsoil entrance.

Our days in Germany, were so totally awesome . . . when we broke camp, for the next destination, Dad said, "From here on, you must be on your best behavior, Sweetie. People, will be watching you. You may not see them but we are here in Europe, for them to see you." I was puzzled, yet, as always, Dad's word was law.

We drove through Austria, and took in Brenner Pass, near Innsbruck, on our way to Italy. How could I possibly know, the fullness of what he had told me? I decided, to look for people . . . looking for me!

Cynthia.

Chapter 9

We pulled into a beautiful camp; hear Pisa, Italy, for our Roman holiday. Mum and Dad, decided first to see Venice, because the day of the "observation," as they put it, was three days away. A swift little boat, took us from our port, out into the waters of Venice, we had a gondola ride, down the Grand Canal and then set off, on foot, touring this romantic, surreal city, which appeared only to sit atop, the Italian waters.

The building bottoms seemed perched, upon the water. Our walking tour, included, such sights, but not limited to . . . the famous prison bridge of Sais, the bustling Rialto Bridge, with its many shops of commerce, upon it. San Marco Square, the churches and the museums. We watched master glass blowers, making beautiful glassware and dined al fresco, at one of the sidewalk cafes.

I never wanted to leave Venice, I wished to live there . . . but that was not meant to be. On day two, in Italy, Dad drove us into Pisa, for sightseeing . . . along the highway, stood the masterpieces of Roman water movement . . . the Roman aqueducts. Dad, of course, explained why they were built and how they functioned, saying, "Without water, people would die!" That would be his first speech, on the importance of water, as life's sustenance.

Finally, into view, came the strangest sight, a round, gothic Roman Tower, the leaning tower of Pisa. I said, "Daddy, can we go on it?" He said, "That's why we're here sweetie!" We had to wait again, just as at King Ludwig's, Dream Castle, for the guides to clear the tower, for our ascent, up the hundreds and hundreds of stairs, which spiraled inside the tower . . . to the top!

Each of the six levels, above the entrance level, had pass-through openings, so one could see from each level, the grounds and views of the area. At the top, there were only two people, left in the tower with us, a Mummy, in her yellow dress and her daughter, in red shorts and white top, with long flowing dark hair.

I tried to talk with the girl, but she only spoke Italian, I only spoke English. What a sight at the top! I remember looking over the edge and feeling like I was falling off . . . I stuck close to Mum and Dad, so that I would not fall off.

On the way back to our beautiful campground, under tall evergreens, with pine needle carpets underneath, in Pisa, we stopped, at a fishing village and bought the "catch du jour," which Dad cooked for us, back at camp.

The camp was Terrenia, Italy, very near Pisa. After dinner, Dad took me for a walk, just he and I, he told me, "Tomorrow . . . is a very important day in your life. You are going to have be on your BEST behavior."

He went on to explain, that a man called, "Pope," in a white priest's robe, the highest priest of the Catholic Church, "named Paul the sixth," would be watching me inside the Vatican and on the grounds. He told me I was the 'Golden Child' and the Pope knew it and had requested that I, "The child," be brought, to observe, "After First Holy Communion, while still seven years old." He went on, to tell me, it was a great honor and never to forget about it.

Well, he wasn't kidding! The day in Rome, started with us taking in the tourist sights, of the Roman Forum, the Coliseum, the Victor Emmanuel Monument and tomb of the Unknown Soldier and the Pictorial Column, on our way to the Vatican, promptly at three p.m.

All the sights were cleared of tourists, for our visits; Even, St. Peter's, Basilica, at the Vatican. Walking through the front courtyard, past the fountain, Dad told me to, "Look, up! at that window, Cindy and wave, to the Pope!"

There he was, a man, in his white robe and beanie, peering down at us! He did not wave, instead, he nodded and raised his right hand and gave the sign of the cross blessing.

The Swiss Guard arrived to usher us in. Inside, a Cardinal had a pair of July birthstone rosaries, which Pope Paul VI, had blessed and sent down, for me. He had black rosaries, for Dad and Billy and crystal rosaries, for Mum. Our tour guide soon came and told Dad, "No photos, please, today, it must not be."

Dad put the camera away and we had the Basilica, completely to ourselves, not another tourist in sight. We were shown its splendor, over about two hours and the last stop was the Pieta. Dad said, "Sweetie, what do you notice about Jesus and his mother, Mary?" I said, "He's small and she's big!" "Right!" he said.

She looked so sad, holding him in her arms. Tears came into my eyes . . . he was dead, in her arms! "Time, to go! . . ." Dad said. Four Swiss Guard came and took us, out a side door, back to the main courtyard. By this time, hundreds of people were waiting, to be let in, as it had been our private audience, for two full hours.

"Mission Accomplished!" Dad told Mum, she just nodded, "Yes Bill, thanks be to God, we did it!" Something changed in me that day; I now had a true connection, to my Roman Catholic "Mecca," and its leader, the Pope. I felt a happiness and peace I'd never known. That peace would be my best friend, through all the days of my life, to come. I felt bad, that it was about me being, "A Golden Child," and, I wondered, why Billy, wasn't one . . .

The next morning, we broke camp and were headed for the Swiss Alps. As we left Italy, we saw the Apian Way, near Rome. Dad said, "Say goodbye to Italy!"

We drove a long way, through the Swiss Alps, taking in all the scenic vistas and of course, the hairpin turns. I was scared to death, we'd go careening . . . off the road! We never did. Instead, we arrived in the beautiful town, of Ponte Teresa, on Lake Lugano. We set up camp and then went into town, to eat at a beautiful sidewalk cafe, near the Lugano fountain. The next day, July 28, 1967, Mum made arrangements at a town bakery, for a birthday cake, which would be shared, at lunchtime, at the campground, with a little Roman girl, named Aurnella, who was on holiday, in the next tent, with her family.

The cake read, "Happy Birthday, Aurnella and Cindy!" We both shared the same birthday! And age of eight, together The rest of the day, we swam and played, with the other children, at the campsite. At one point, I remember, I was lying, on the bottom of Lake Lugano, in about three feet of water, holding my breath. I looked up, through the water and saw the Sun and its rays and crystal prisms shining, through the cold water.

It reminded me of that crystal hallway, I had traveled, when I had left my body, at the time I nearly died, of bilateral Pneumonitis. I stayed on the bottom and counted to sixty that was all I could take. Aurnella, reached down to help me up. I had her address, in Rome and wrote to her twice, but I never received a letter back. I'll never forget her . . . or the fun, or our birthdays, spent, at beautiful Lake Lugano, Switzerland . . . together.

Cynthia.

Chapter 10

And so, our last sight in Switzerland was to be, the beautiful Swiss Miniature at Lake Lugano. It was a grand walking tour, with a small train, surrounding the perimeter. I had heard of Gulliver's Travels and had a chance to walk amongst, miniature buildings, of the many Swiss villages and castles, which were exact duplicates, scaled down, to enjoy over concrete paths, joining them.

All of a sudden, Dad said, "Sweetie, go over to that castle and pretend you are the queen and it is yours and you have to address your subjects, on the topic of war!" "What!?!" I said. "Just go over there and look very serious and pretend; you have to make a great big decision, for your country!" He waited and guided me through many poses, then he finally said, "Got it! That's the pose, now hold it!" He took the shot.

As I look back on it now, I can understand his reasoning. That night back at camp, over dinner, Dad announced that tomorrow, we'd be driving all day and night, straight through, to Calais, France, to again, board the English Channel Ferry, to return to the beautiful White Cliffs of Dover.

Our last daylight in Switzerland, that next morning, brought a stop, by picturesque, Lake Lucerne, back through the Swiss Alps, passing through the village, near Saint Goddard Pass and a quick stop at a nearby cathedral. We reached Calais, early the next morning, after having driven back, over different roads, than the approach, to see scenery, from the car.

We pulled back into the Epping Forest Campground, in London and pitched camp for the night. The next days ride, would be home, to bonnie Scotland. Dad had only two more days leave, so time was of the essence. It was cold when we pulled into Eidenborough, to tour the castle. Again, all tourists were cleared, so that we could have an exclusive, private, viewing.

How grandiose and gothic, this ancient Celtic castle was. We were taken to a special section of the castle, because we were the Gunns. Dad told me, as we lagged behind, just he and I, soaking in the sight, of Scotland's Crown Jewels, "Sweetie, someday I will tell you who you are and just why, we are here, amongst the crown jewels of Scotland, but not now." I had seen some of the crown jewels in London, at the beginning of our journey but the ones . . . that the public could see, yet . . . this was different.

We were given access, to see all of Scotland's Crown Jewels, deep within the secret recesses, of beautiful Eidenborough Castle. I wondered . . . "Who am I!?! Why did all these things happen . . . what does Dad mean by, 'someday I will tell you who you are . . .'" All those thoughts passed, when we announced, we wanted to get ice cream. "Come on," Dad said, "Let's go, let's get ice cream, before we drive home to "Onich." We got into the car and drove away from the castle. I couldn't wait for that ice cream.

Yet still, I wondered, what the whole tour of Great Britain and Europe, was about . . . I soon dismissed it, for I knew someday, when the time was exactly right, Dad would tell me, all he meant.

On the last day of Dad's leave, back home, we took a ride to downtown Dunoon. First, it was every Sunday, we went to the Simon Lake, in the Holy Loch, by boat and walked the gangway, for mass, to the chapel on the ship and of course, we had our gourmet breakfast, the family tradition, in the officer's wardroom.

Once again being waited on, by young, Navy men, in white dinner jackets, who seated and served us, at table, with fine white linen cloths and napkins, which they placed gently on our laps, upon arrival. First, the water glasses were filled and then, our orders were taken. Mum, Dad and Billy would choose various courses at brunch. I would have the same thing, every Sunday, for the two beautiful years, we lived in Scotland. A Belgian waffle, drenched in sweet creamery butter and refined sugar. I would meticulously spread into every chamber, of the waffle.

Fresh squeezed orange juice and chocolate milk. How I loved those Sunday trips, by car, from "Onich," Toward, by Dunoon, through Dunoon and along the shore road, which ran near waters edge, of the Holy Loch, to the stately ship, Simon Lake.

We would always see the tinker camp, by the Loch, they were very poor gypsies. I would get teary eyed, at how they lived, in patchwork shacks. After brunch, we stopped at Westbay, by Dunoon, so we could play, at the camp playground, walk the shore path and view the flower gardens. It was the perfect ending, to Dad's month long leave and the continent, of Europe. I was so very happy, all through our journey, we got along so well and Dad didn't beat Mum, at all. How I hoped, that the beatings, would never again begin, but I did not know.

The next couple of weeks, were all, so very peaceful at "Onich." Billy and I would ride our bikes, all day, on the grounds and Mum and Dad would watch us. I would spend hours, past the gate wall, on the sand stone rocks, at the Firth of Clyde, directly past the wall.

Low tide, was my favorite time, to play there. I would collect snails and tap their shells, to make them hide inside. I played with the seaweeds and the rocks and made quite a rock collection, for myself, all the while, knowing, that our tour of duty, in bonnie Scotland, was coming to a close, very soon.

In the fall of '67, we went back to Ardlui Campground, at Loch Lomond. We rode the, "Maid of the Loch," cruise ship and of course stopped at, "Rest and be Thankful," the beautiful mountain pass between Dunoon and Glasgow. Our last big car trip of the fall season was, to Loch Linne, at Oban. We didn't have time to ride the Mull ferry, which disappointed me. How Dad's little, as he said, "Scottish-American Princess," loved her motherland.

I was torn, between wishing to live in Scotland forever . . . or going back to the States and being reunited, with the family. Once again, it was, "Uncle Sam," who decided.

Cynthia.

Chapter 11

With Europe behind us, we pulled into "Onich," I was in a state of extreme calm, as we had no beating occur, in Europe. Of course, soon they began again, as that party circuit reemerged.

In February of '68, we needed to go for shots, to return to the United States. It was in Scotland, that I began to have chronic ear infections and Strep throats. Navy doctors didn't believe in removing tonsils or adenoids, so I suffered . . . beginning to know, what physical pain was.

What is physical pain? It's when you hurt, you bodily feel, whatever is not going well, with the body. Some physical pain is brought on, by illness and disease. Other physical pain is, inflicted on us, by others. I began to understand the difference, between terror and fear and being injured, or not well.

On the day of the shots, I sat on the exam table, as the doctor came toward me, with the needle, I freaked out and ran outside the infirmary. Dad came outside and threatened to beat me . . . if I didn't take my shots. I told him how sick I was, the last time, in the US. Again, he threatened. I said, "I don't care what you do to me, I'm not having shots, so go ahead . . . and beat me!"

He was stunned; I had made my first true stand. He calmly, reached into his pocket and took out a crisp new, one hundred dollar bill. "If you take your shots, without a peep, you can have this hundred dollar bill!" I agreed, for I already knew, the value of money.

Back on the exam table, I took my shots, however, I did cry. When we all got into the car, Dad said, "Because you weren't silent, you're only going to get half . . . fifty dollars! I took the fifty and put it in my pocket; he had, after all, struck a fair deal.

We went to "Onich," to the packers. I was hopeful, that our return to the States and tour of duty, next, at the Subase, New London-Groton, Connecticut, would bring change in terms of the beatings. Again, Pan Am flew us across the pond. The car was sent ahead and delivered to us, at the JFK airport. We piled in for the ride, to Nanna and Dziadzi's house. I was so happy, to be going back to Mum's family, in Connecticut. As we entered the state, I counted each exit, until finally, exit 81 East, Norwichtown.

We pulled in late in the afternoon. All the Connecticut family, were present, except Father Walter. We did a lengthy meet and greet, after two long years, without them. After the meal, it was time for bed. My place was to share, the bed of my cousin, Cheryl, seven years my senior.

Downstairs, the adults were enjoying cocktails and conversation, I was a bit fearful, Dad would beat Mum. It did not happen while there.

The next day, I went to Samuel Huntington School, in Norwichtown, to enter the US third grade, even though I'd left the fifth grade, in Scotland. I was just where I needed to be, academically now.

I entered the classroom, as I did all the others, from Hilton Baptist Day school to this point, remembering Dad's famous quote, "You're the daughter of a naval officer, a child of the world, if you don't make friends, you're going to be awfully lonely." I scanned all the faces, at the desks and was placed directly behind a pretty redheaded girl, named Diane.

She kept turning around and telling me what was next. We became good friends, in class, at recess, the whole nine! When June came and school ended, I again had to say goodbye, to a friend, to Diane and all the new friends, for we were going to be moving, in the summer, to Uncasville, Connecticut.

Dad had found a TLC special and fixer-upper and he made it a palace. The unpacking and setup was as usual, long and arduous. Dad put up a round swimming pool and the summer was complete. We enjoyed Holly Hill Drive, that first summer. Dad only beat Mum once or twice, but each night, since that first, at four years old, I prayed, "Dear God, please don't let Daddy beat Mummy tonight, please I beg of you, I love you, Goodnight!"

Most nights, God could prevent Dad, but I came to understand, that on certain nights, not even God, could stop my father's ire. I never blamed God, when Dad didn't listen to him, I just accepted the outcomes.

The first day of the fourth grade, at the Mohegan School, in Uncasville, couldn't come soon enough. Mrs. Andrews was the teacher, an elegant lady, tall and with short black hair, in beautiful dresses, who wore a sweater, always, clipped over her shoulders and of course, her reading glasses cinched with a pearl chain, around her neck.

I made friends fast, as always. I would stay in at recess, just to talk with her. I learned she had arthritis in her shoulders. Soon, I was helping her with strenuous tasks . . . eraser clapping, blackboard cleaning and the like. We became fast friends. She suggested, I join the square dancing club, since I had told her of my Highland Dancing, in bonnie Scotland.

The square dancing was conducted by a Mrs. Jean Wydra, of Norwich, a woman, with a large family, who could call like any pro, in Nashville! Mum was charged with making my dress, a pink gingham number. She put four yards of material, exactly, drawn at the skirt, so that when I whirled around, in my horsehair slip, the gingham petticoat was visible and the skirt stood out, at horizontal level.

When school ended that June of '68, for the summer, Dad announced we'd be going to see his Mum, Gran, his sister, Aunt Belly and the girls, the cousins, Nancy Jo, Virginia and Laine. He said, "I have twenty five days leave again this summer, we're going to Alabama . . . via upstate New York and Michigan!"

I thought that was odd. Mostly, when we headed to Alabama, we went southward, not northwestward, toward Alabama. We set out on July 1, and went to the Eastman Kodak Mansion and many sights, along the New York leg, of our journey. We were great fort-goers and so of course, every fort along the way, was viewed. Ticonderoga was great fun. There were caverns, I think . . . Howe Caverns, which were my first taste of the underground since the Saltzbergwerks at Bertchesgaten, Germany.

At Howe Caverns, an elevator propelled one downward, into the earth's crust, to walk paths along underground lakes and streams, to view stalactites, from above and stalagmites, which rose from below, due to dripping of stalactites and of course, many beautiful, natural, underground wonders. Unlike the salt mines, the caverns were darker, colder and wetter. It was a chilly damp cold, which was most uncomfortable, since we were wearing summer clothes, below, in about forty two degrees. I was shivering and Mother and Father, took turns warming me up.

The next day, we were off to Niagara Falls. The American Falls were in the process, of being damned up, with no overflow, because the government was to reinforce them, with concrete, due to erosion. We only saw the Canadian side and local museums. I remember seeing the wax people museum. It was a bit scary. We drove and drove, to Detroit, Michigan, where we had a beautiful, posh, hotel suite, for a four night stay.

We toured the Ford Motor Plant, a steel factory and the Henry Ford Museum. The factories, were not my favorite things, the museum amazed me. I couldn't get enough. Of course, after experiencing Europe and Great Britain, I had been schooled, to take in every sight and person to behold.

My favorite part of this vacation was living, in the hotel suite. We were camping, the summer before, so it was a welcome change. At the swimming pool, for four wonderful days, in a row, I swam and played with a little boy, nine years old, named Michael . . . Jackson.

I was going to be nine on July 28th, so we were very close, in age. Michael, had many brothers and a couple of sisters, he told me. I only had Billy. Michael and I talked about that and how we felt about our siblings. Michael and I had so much fun, the most I've ever had playing with a little boy.

His father, Joseph, would come to the pool, to collect Michael and his siblings, because Michael would have to go to work! Michael's face would change, from happy to sad, at the time he needed to go and work, but over and over the next three more days, we'd get back to our fun and fooling around and horseplay, with towels, at poolside, only to again . . . until the day before I had to leave I would watch him, get so sad, when his father, Joseph, would call him away, from our playtime, to go to work!

I said to my Daddy, "Why does Michael, have to go to work! He's a kid like me . . . I don't go to work!" Dad said he'd explain it to me, in a couple of days.

When that day came, we were driving through a place called Gary, Indiana. Dad searched and searched the neighborhoods. Soon, he found a small house and pulled up in front and stopped. He said, "Sweetie, remember that little boy you like? And played with so much? Michael Jackson?" I said, "Yes!" "Well Sweetie, this is the house, he and his brothers and sisters, live in." "I said . . . no sir! It's way too small, Daddy!" Again, he said, "I'm telling you, this is the house, they all use to live in!" and the reason your friend, Michael, had to go to work and stop playing, with you is because, he is going to be famous!"

"What do you mean . . . famous?!? I said. My father said, "You will hear about the JACKSON 5, on the radio." "I will?" I said. "Well Sweetie that WILL BE MICHAEL and his brothers on the radio." "I said, "No, it won't!" He said, "Yes, it will, (well he said,) didn't Michael tell you who he was? And what he's doing?" I said, "No! We were just . . . playing together and I really miss him!"

Dad said, "Someday, you will meet him again, when you are older, but for right now . . . just know you were meant to meet him. When you are older, I will explain why." "Okay!" I said, and dismissed it . . . because if Dad said it, it was golden . . . law!

This was just a beautiful time in my life. I was very happy. That fall, of 1968, was going so good, no beatings in about a month. Then one Saturday morning, I heard Mum, crying. I thought . . . Oh no! He's going to beat her in the day!

As I moved closer to their room, I heard Dad say, "What do you expect? Cheryl's good for nothing. So she's pregnant, so were you and your mother!" Now, I knew what pregnancy was, but not how it happened. I entered their room . . . they were taken aback.

I said, "Who's pregnant!" Thinking Mum, Nanna and Cheryl were pregnant. They said in unison, "Cheryl," and my father went on to describe, "She's on her way to Maryland, with Harry, to get married."

I walked out thinking, now Cheryl, will be a Mummy and she won't live at Nanna's anymore . . . which made me very sad.

Cynthia.

Chapter 12

When Christmas Eve came, we went to Norwichtown, for Wigilia, the traditional Polish meal and prayers, with the individual sentiments, spoken over broken wafers. Each family member presents their bread, to the others, until all have shared messages of love, to each other. From the oldest to the youngest, it must be done.

Although it was nice, Cheryl wasn't there, because she was pregnant. She was being shunned, even though, we were not Amish. I did not understand this, because as I thought, having a baby, was a happy time. Soon, in the January, of 1969, we heard that Cheryl had finally been married, at Harry's parent's house, by justice of the peace and not months earlier, in Maryland.

On a rainy, raw day, in April, Mum took me to that house to see the new baby, Mark. I was immediately drawn to him. Very soon, after Cheryl, Harry and baby Mark moved, into a small basement flat, in Lisbon, Connecticut.

In the fullness of time, it was Mark's first Birthday. They had relocated to a Cape Cod house, a small one, in Norwichtown, Connecticut. At the party, I wore my square dance dress, for the occasion. Mum and Dad, went to the Submarine Base, for Dad's own, officer retirement party. It was March 29, 1970 to be exact.

A blizzard ensued and so I spent two days at Nanna's. My worst fears were realized, those two days later, when Mum came to pick me up! She donned her sunglasses, again and didn't come into her parent's house, to collect me. She had been beaten, probably the night of Mark and Dad's party. I asked her, "Mummy? Why does Daddy beat you? Yes, you drink alcohol, but so does he and so do all the grownups. Why are you the only one, who gets beaten?"

No answer from her, only tears, streaming down her cheeks. That day, I vowed to myself, to die if necessary, for her and to try and stop him . . . whenever I could. I didn't speak to Dad, for two or three days. He tried to conversate with me; I would turn and walk away, which made him furious!

When I decided to talk to him I said, "I don't like you anymore!" He said nothing and went for a drive . . . what I meant, from the pit of my soul was, "I don't like you anymore, because only Mummy gets beaten, for drinking alcohol!"

Something changed that day. Dad was put on notice that I would not . . . put up, without a fight . . . all well and good. He had taught me from a young age, "Be aware of your surroundings, be a good girl, be Scottish, be a Gunn, aut pax, aut bellum, either peace or war!" The Gunn, family credo . . . ahah! I embraced all of his messages, with a new fervor.

He had taught us, to be good yet he was being . . . bad! I couldn't understand how he could be so opposite, his own messages. One day, at Cheryl's, in Lisbon, she explained how baby Mark was conceived and born, how he was in her belly, for nine months and the entire process, of how she had gotten pregnant, in the first place.

Huh! I had a few young boys, that I was sweet on, school boys, at the tender ages and of course, Michael . . . whom I had met in the summer of 1968 . . . swimming . . . but, I couldn't imagine, at almost eleven, letting any boy, do that to me, ever.

This would be the first summer I watched everyone, with new and improved, eyes . . . . eyes that would look, ears that would listen and a mind, that would decide, who was right or wrong. When Father Walter returned for his summer stay, at the Misquamicut Family Beach Cottage, I noticed that even HE . . . drank alcohol . . . and I watched him flirt, with a woman, named Pauline.

How could that be?!? He was supposed to be a Priest! Another Christ! . . . as the nuns, in Scotland, had taught us. Well, the days and nights at that cottage, were so fun and relaxed. There, Dad could not beat Mum. The ocean sand and surf are something; everyone should have a chance to enjoy.

My cousin, Ricky, Cheryl's younger brother, two years my junior was my pal. We'd ride our Styrofoam, half-body boards, over and through the undertow . . . fearlessly! At night, we'd burn sparklers and light fire crackers, before going to the amusement rides, next to the Misquamicut, Rhode Island, state beach.

I remember sitting on the Ferris wheel and loving it, when it stopped, at the top. We'd look out, over the ocean and I'd recall, just how big the world was. Much larger now, because I had seen Europe, the US, the British Isles and I'd remembered, all the flights and the car trips and all the people, that I'd seen and their different customs, art forms and languages.

I would ask God, "When will there be peace in my life . . . in my home?" I knew the answers would come . . . for he always answers prayers, as Mum taught me, "When God answers . . . honey . . . its yes, no, or not now!" The not now answer, always seemed to prevail, but I never gave up hope, in God.

That summer, I began to spend more time, with Cheryl and her new family. I became a sort of a Mother's helper, at the age of eleven, nearly. I would cuddle, kiss and care for Mark. She taught me how to feed, bathe, clothe and change his diapers. I played with him, for hour upon hour.

Soon, I was spending my weekends there, whenever I could, even though I'd return home, to find Mum had often been beaten, many times, when I was away. That fall, of 1970, brought a new weapon into my hands . . . the BB gun. Dad was a collector of guns and a hunter. He and Billy, would go deer and squirrel hunting.

Dad set up can targets for me and made me shoot, also songbirds, in flight . . . I hated killing the tiny birds, but he insisted I hit moving targets. Although I am right handed, he taught me, I was left-eyed. This was the eye that hit the target, moving or stationary, every time.

He started to have me speed read, with a device that flashed words, from behind a plastic shuttle. He insisted . . . that I learn how to handle and care for, the guns. To respect and know the Constitutional right, to bear arms. Read and understand the Constitution and above all, "Honey, if it comes to kill or be killed, you kill, every time. You must protect your life, be aware of your surroundings!"

Mum, began to have me help, with household chores. Laundry, dusting, ironing, cleaning bathrooms and she had me start making my own bed and cleaning my room. Mum was of course, the art lover as always, which included all of the arts, we so enjoyed. She had me start John Thompson's piano lesson courses, with a tutor, in addition to all the other art projects that, I was working on, from a small girl.

Dad established an allowance of money, a new one, for my new chores and responsibilities. He took me, to the Navy Credit Union and insisted, I bank, most of my money, including Birthday and Christmas gift money. I was becoming more independent minded and they were letting me, although, I knew, I was always being watched.

Cynthia.

Chapter 13

That year of 1970, was a very interesting year for me, indeed. At the beginning of the year, right after the Wigilia, I decided that I would do an annual review, so all throughout the year; I tried to recall everything, good, bad or indifferent and see what I could do, differently, in the New Year.

I had recalled that in the year before, I was taught many things, but now, in this new year, I was taught the Constitution, right to bear arms, true money management, speed reading, piano, baby care and responsibility of chores . . . increasing. I remembered too, that there was that big world out there. I rededicated myself to protecting Mum, at all costs and to be better than the year before.

I was most enthralled, when the Astronaut, had landed on the moon, the summer before, because . . . I am the moon . . . in Greek, Cynthia. That event, which I recalled, in July of 1969, connected me to my celestial guide, always there, a constant light in the sky, Cynthia, the moon. I studied our solar system and the arrangement of the planets, in God's creation . . . so big . . . and yet, so small, with all their accomplishments.

Dad retired from the Navy, after those 23 years, as Admiral Rickover's, personal assistant and I remember him saying, "The Admiral said, 'take a year off, then be ready . . . for another adventure'" That summer, of '70, especially, was the calmest, most loving time, our family would ever enjoy, yet the whole year was good and peaceful, for the most part.

Dad was like I had never . . . seen him before, suddenly not uptight, more relaxed and happy, instead. He did not beat Mum at all that summer, because he was around, no need for bitterness and paranoia, about imaginary affairs and flirtations, over and over. This continued and we had a wonderful holiday season, of Thanksgiving and Christmas, that year, as well.

That fall, in addition, Billy had gotten his drivers license and sported around in the '65 Chevy, Biscayne Sedan, or the '68 Mustang, that Mum and Dad owned. He started a job, with Lehigh Oil Company of Norwich, as a gas attendant. The price point was 29.9¢ a gallon. As I said before, a peace we had never before known, came upon our family and our home. I was so grateful, that my prayers, on that Ferris wheel, were answered.

Before the campaign year of 1970 Dad got a call from the Admiral, "Gunn, you need to help a man named Bill, build his Jetport, in Connecticut, here's his number, join the campaign!" Just as before, Dad did as Rickover told him and so, my father became, that gentleman's campaign manager. What a great year, it was turning out to be. Everything was as it should be . . . we spent the summer at the Mopsic yacht, at Terra Mar, Yacht and Tennis Club, of Old Saybrook, Connecticut. We worked to elect Mr. Bill, who wanted to build the Jetport and we had the first Christmas, without a beating. Life looked so good . . . I thought it was and then it happened.

I was home sick one day in 1971. I heard, "Bill the Admiral's on the phone!" my mother's voice. To my chagrin, he was back in our lives. I didn't want Rickover in our life, because it always meant trouble, at home. Why did it mean trouble? Because, Dad had spent those 23 at Rickovers beck and call, all hours of day or night, he had to go all over the east coast, at the drop of a hat, out to sea, so much . . . it seemed he was never home, to far away places . . . he would go to investigations, for months on end, to try and find causes for things, such as the Scorpion and the Thresher disasters. Ah! it was all too much on Mum and we kids. The demands of the naval officer and here it goes . . . again!

Wife, children, home life and happiness, again, will be put behind the Admiral?!? Mum cried and begged, "Please Bill! No! Take a job here, don't go to Pennsylvania, we're happy, you have your retirement, the kids are finally settled. I don't want to move, ever again!"

As I sat eating, my Campbell's Beef with Vegetable and Barley soup, I began to sob. They didn't think I heard them, but I did! Dad went on, "My mind is made up, I'm taking the job!" . . . "What job?!?" I called out. "Mind your Goddamned business, I'll tell you when I'm damned good and ready!" he snapped.

Oh! My worst nightmare . . . The horrible Dad was back! He continued to be mean to Mum and me, for the first time, since he had retired, basically and I became physically sick, and threw up the soup. "Quit your bull shit, Cindy!" he screamed.

Before Billy got home, he sat me down with Mum, at my side. She comforted me. "Just sit there and don't say a word, remember children should be seen and not heard. Do you understand me! Don't take and don't make, any of your snot nosed comments, or I'll beat your ass!"

I knew it would be bad, but not how bad. He said, "The Admiral wants me to build a power plant on the Susquehanna River, in Middletown, Pennsylvania, it's called Three Mile Island and we're moving soon, so pack your shit and get ready!"

Ugh! Within a few days, Dad left. When he returned, he had a brand new company car and all the perks any executive could want. We had no choice and no say in the matter. Billy, wanted to stay in Connecticut, so he could finish his fourth year, until 1972 and graduate with his high school class, at St. Bernard's, in Uncasville, Connecticut.

After many arguments and much turmoil, Mom acquiesced and said, she'd stay behind, with us kids, for another school year, so Billy could graduate with his friends, he had made. So the plan became, Dad commuting and living in Pennsylvania and coming home, six hours through the Pocono's, every weekend. Dad came home every weekend, for a few months . . .

In the New Year 1972, it became every two or three weeks, then only once a month. Billy graduated in June and Mum broached the subject, "Bill, we can move to Pennsylvania now." Dad shut it down; he insisted now, that we had to stay behind so I could graduate the eighth grade, with my class at St. Joseph's School, in downtown, Norwich, Connecticut "Remember, Cindy's afraid of drugs. Let's not take her out of that school just now, let her stay there and start fresh, in high school, in Pennsylvania!" he said.

Well yes, I had chosen to go Catholic Junior High grades, so now this, became the reason. He reminded me of my crying at the end of the sixth grade, because I had just seen the movie, "Go Ask Alice" In it, the girl moved to a new town, went to a new junior high school, went to a party, was given drug laced soda and then began, the downward spiral, into drugs, resulting in her death!

It made me deathly afraid, all that could happen to me, if I went to the Montville Junior High School, a known pothead school. Remembering me, being adamant, to go to St. Joseph's instead, for junior high, became Dad's reason, for Mum and myself and Billy, to stay in Connecticut. "You and the kids stay in Connecticut, another year, for Cindy's sake!" Mum, reluctantly agreed and went into a deeper depression.

She began to drink heavily, all week, or for weeks on end, until the few times, Dad returned. She manage to, "Sober Up . . ." only for his brief visits One day, while home from school, I heard Mum and her friend Martie, in the living room, "Celene, he's still your husband, forget about, all Bill's women, you are still his wife!"

Mum just cried, all the more. I didn't know what on earth Martie meant. As I folded the paper bags from the Subase Commissary, the message on the side, stunned me, "Navy wife, toughest job in the Navy!" I understood it! . . . But now the reason would become, Three Mile Island!

Cynthia.

Chapter 14

After two months of hell, with Dad not wanting us to move to Pennsylvania, after all, the day was set, July 28, 1973; my fourteenth birthday. We went to Nanna's house early, where we said goodbye to all the Connecticut relatives and now, Billy!

He refused to move away, because he had one year of Mohegan Community College, in Norwich, Connecticut, under his belt. Nanna agreed, he could live there and stay in that college. As Mum, Dad and I got into her new Chevy Caprice, for the long ride to Middletown, Pennsylvania; I dreaded what I would have to deal with, as the only child left, at home.

Another hardship occurred, that day . . . as my second menstrual period, ever.

It came in June, the first time, after I had got out of the eighth grade and it was brutal! All I could think about, whenever I bled, was the speech, Cheryl had given me, from my first cycle, "Be careful now, that you can get pregnant, watch out for my step-father, Richard, he may try to have sex with you, because he had molested me since I was three, when I bled at twelve and told Nanna, she took me to live at her house!"

Well, Cheryl's warning was one, I'll always be grateful for, because I never wanted to end up pregnant before a Catholic Church Marriage, like she, Mum and Nanna had. I also firmly believed, what the nuns had taught me, earlier, to save myself, for marriage.

The trip was a nightmare; Dad was like a caged bear. He bitched all the way and threatened to take us, back to Connecticut, several times if we ever gave him, any shit. He would pass, several tractor trailer trucks, at once . . . on Route 209 in the Pocono's. Like a madman driving, he seemed not to care, if we all died, in a car crash!

It was evident, he didn't want Mum and I, to move to Pennsylvania, I could not understand why? . . . He was so mad! We had after all, waited two years to join him. We arrived at the house in Middletown, on 916 Oberlin Road, after having a meal, in the Italian Restaurant, downtown Hershey, Pennsylvania. At dinner, I marveled at the Kiss Street lights, as I blew out my birthday candle, on my single slice of cake.

The house was owned by GPU, the company Dad worked for. It was filthy! Mum and I worked our tails off, making it livable. As we'd vacuum, we'd hear clicking noises, every few feet. When we went to clean out the bag, dozens of black bobby pins fell, on the carpet and were stuck, in the hose.

That night at dinner, Mum asked Dad, why the house was so filthy, before we got there and who's hairpins, were clogging the vacuum? He got extremely pissed off and said, "Norm's damned girlfriend!" Norm had been his roommate the last two years, before we arrived, so it was a logical explanation The subject was closed.

Very soon, Dad took Mum and I, to a department store in town, called the Big M. He took us to the back office. At the main desk, was a bookkeeper, "This is Maria and she's going to give Cindy a job, Saturdays and Sundays, sacking at the registers."

Mum and I were dumbfounded. He didn't ask, he just told. The woman set the pay, at three dollars an hour, under the table. I started the following weekend. Big M, was a blast! . . . for I had her twin daughters, Melissa and Marisa, my same age, as my new ready-made friends and bagging co-workers. Soon, I was sleeping over their house, on weekends, for work.

When the ice hockey season started for the Hershey Bears, Dad drove Mum and me to the arena. The valets parked, the car and we entered and took our season seats, at center ice, directly behind the team. "These are the best seats, in the house and we have them for the season, on the company!" Dad announced.

About three sections away and halfway up the side, Maria and her four children, sat. All through the hockey season and the Bears triumphant bid, at the Calder Cup, the twins and I continued to bond. After every game, we went to the hallway, outside the locker room below, to see the players, after they showered and left. All three of us were hung-up on a player named Jim Hrycuik, we would swoon, as if he were a rock star! He was drop dead gorgeous!

In January of '74, something very disturbing happened. Mum had a new, experimental surgery, at the Hershey Medical Center, a total hip replacement, of the left hip. Since she had moved to Pennsylvania and Dad was never home, at every single night, we, she and I were always alone, mostly at night. We would ask Dad, why he wouldn't come home, at night and he would say that he had problems, at Three Mile Island and had to work there late . . . habitually!

When Mum complained, "Bill, you're never home," he'd storm out and not return, for a few days, saying, "Don't call me! I'll be home when I get here!" She was miserable again, just as she'd been, when he worked for the Admiral! In the Navy! And the Atomic Energy Commission! Oh, my God!

Well, sadly, occasionally, Mum would get, drunk on her own and if he saw, that she had been drinking, the beatings were back! Oh, my God! He was so mean, that he even threatened to shoot our St. Bernard dog, Baby, that we had gotten in Connecticut, when I was in the Catholic junior high school, because the neighbor, was complaining, that Baby broke her chain and was trampling their flowers, again and again. Well, we were mortified, that Dad would shoot Baby!..if Baby would get off the chain!

Dad never had liked Baby, because she wasn't a Dachshund. He was against, anything that he didn't want, or couldn't control. One particular day, visiting Mum in the Hospital, she said, "Bill, why didn't you bring Cindy yesterday?" I said, "Because he leaves me home alone at night and never came home yesterday, at all!" Ugh! Her stay lasted three weeks, the worst three weeks of my life!

I had to get myself up, get myself, my clothes, my lunch, care for Baby, get to the bus and get back home and alone, every night, at the end of a dead end road, with no family and nasty neighbors. I was scared to death. He left me that way.

Something very strange happened, the night before, Mum came home. Dad said, "You'll see your mother tomorrow, tonight we're taking Marie and the kids, out to dinner." I said nothing. Instantly, I had a dreadful feeling, but didn't know why..

When we got to their house, Maria Trini, Melissa, Marisa and Steven, got in the car. Maria scooted in, right next to Dad, with Trini at the door. Melissa, Marisa and I, sat in the second seat; Steven sat in the rear seat, of the station wagon. I watched, as Dad put his arm around Maria and left it there.

I knew our families were friends, even at church, for Saturday masses, which her husband Ralph, also attended. Their family in one row and the three of us, in another row, but this was unorthodox! Mum in the hospital and Ralph at home and the rest of us, were going out to eat?!?

When I tapped Dad on the shoulder and said, "Why do you have your arm that way?" He reached back and punched my face, bloodying my nose, "Mind your own fucking business and if you breathe a word of this, to your mother, I'll kill you!"

Cynthia.

Chapter 15

That night, I took the beating of a lifetime! I was now a clone of my own mother! Two black eyes, a bloody nose and badly beaten. Dad brought Mum home, the next day and I stayed behind. He got her in the house and left, not returning for a week. He never called.

Mum was on crutches, after three weeks of traction, an invalid practically. I spent that week, home from school, feeding, toileting, bathing and taking care of her. She was physically and emotionally a wreck! I said nothing, about why I had been beaten.

She'd ask, "What did you do to make Daddy beat you?" I just told her, "He thinks I was bad, but I wasn't." I began to hate Three Mile Island, for it made Dad meaner and more ruthless, than even Admiral Rickover had. I would pray at night, "Dear God, please do something to Three Mile Island, so we can leave Pennsylvania!"

That prayer, became my most earnest request, for I knew, it was a lot to ask of God, to stop a nuclear power plant, from ruining our lives! On the eyes of March, I awoke at about 3:00 a.m., from a sound sleep and took the earplugs, out of my ears, which cut the road noise, of the interstate, at our side yard.

All the lights in the kitchen were on. On the way to their bedroom, I noticed the house was disheveled, as if an intruder had ransacked, the place. I walked toward the hallway, which led to their bedroom. Inside, in the light, cast from the TV set, I saw Dad, go into the closet shelf, take down the home security pistol, put the clip in the butt and put it up to Mum's head!

I screamed, at the top of my lungs, "Are you fucking crazy? If you kill her, you're going to have to kill me too . . . because I'm going to tell them, you did it!" Mum woke up and was scared to death!

He, calmly, stoically, took out the clip, put the items back on the closet shelf, shoved me as he walked by, not saying a word. I knew then, that I had just saved both of our lives, by the grace of God.

The day of St. Patrick, March 14, 1974, at about 6:00 a.m., through those same earplugs, I heard Mum sobbing and again begging, "Please Bill! No!" I got out of my bed and entered the living room, to find Mum, in her nightgown, on the piano bench and Dad; and Maria, on the couch, embracing.

As I entered the room I said, "What is going on here!" He screamed, "Go back to bed!" I screamed louder, "No, I won't go back to bed, I'm staying right here!" I flew to Mums side, at the bench, to console her. Dad and Maria calmly and smugly stated, they were quote, "In Love . . . and we both want divorces, so we can be married!"

Now, all the pieces, of his dastardly puzzle, of the last two years, plus . . . fit into place. They took no questions, only barked their intentions. They left soon after and Dad never again, came home. The months from St. Patty's Day, until school let out in June, were unbearable.

Dad, would show up, on a pay day, throw money on the table, tell Mum to, "go fuck yourself!" and leave. We had to get out of there, but where would we go?!?

At the end of June, the movers came Dad separated his booty, as if he, were a warlord! Post conquers! I had no idea where we would live, until Mum told me, "We're moving near Nanna, in Connecticut" I was relieved, because we were loved and wanted there, all through the years, and so I hoped, for deliverance, from Dad and his evil behavior, the worst of which, was not leaving without Dad, but having to leave, without Baby, our St. Bernard.

I remember wailing at the pit of my soul, as we drove away, from the humane society. Knowing full well, she'd probably be put to sleep, because of Dad and Maria. With that behind us, Mum and I made the last trip, through the Pocono Mountains, to Connecticut.

We first, went to a new apartment complex, behind the Norwich Sheraton, our new address. All our things had been shipped and Nanna made sure, it was ready when we got there. It was a three bedroom apartment, because Billy was supposed to rejoin us there, but he did not. Instead, he moved, into the home and bed, of his fifteen year old girlfriend, Debby, at her parents' approval!

Now, we had Dad in adultery and Billy in fornication, my moral compass was spinning, at the sheer unadulterated evil, I was beholding, as taught by the Roman Catholic Church, Mums heritage and Dads conversion.

I was totally disgusted! Soon, Mums alcohol consumption was, at an all time high and her morals, at an all new, all time low. She'd go out every night, to the local adult hang-out bars and drink a fifth, of Old Grandad, by day. Often times, I'd hear her and the men she'd pick-up, in the throws of lust, in the living room.

I hated all those new, low life, bums, she brought home. Bad enough, we were out of our element, in an apartment and financially struggling, at the same time. I started to hate, her alcohol drinking and the riffraff she attracted and the fact, that we, had sunk, below living in a private home of our own.

Dad would call, two or three times a week and send her money, whenever he damned well pleased. Soon, we were harassed, by bill collectors and the refrigerator was empty. I'd ask Mum, "What are we having to eat?" She'd say, "Ramen noodles, again," and go back to her drunken stupor.

When school started, in the fall of '74, I loved leaving home for the day, like never before. I had slept that summer, at Cheryl's house mostly, for now . . . she had a new baby, Michelle, whom I became the Godmother to in the September, of 1973. I hated leaving Cheryl and Harry's house and the children.

I dreaded going back to Mum, in the apartment and living "Dad's will," of St. Patty's Day, "Maria and her kids, are my new life and my new family!"

In Cheryl's neighborhood, there were boys, across the street, playing basketball, every day, brothers, Bill and Bob and their friend Dave. Dave was gorgeous in my eyes and his personality was even more . . . beautiful! I had begun my first love, unrequited though it was. Bill, the older of the two brothers and Bob, both liked me and wanted to date me, but I only had eyes and a heart for Dave. He was effervescent, he was fun, he loved life, was charming and looked like Richard Gere's, better looking brother!

Soon, Dave's sisters, Diane and Debbie . . . cruised the neighborhood How could I have known, she was the same Diane from the third grade!?! Huh! When I discovered that fact, I took to her instantly and loved Dave, all the more! By the time school opened, I was a fixture, in Dave's car, as his buddy and reunited with Diane.

Life was good; I looked forward to school and Cheryl's neighborhood, for the social and soul soothing atmosphere it gave to me. I was part of something I had friends! I had arrived in adolescence! I could care less, about Dad. He didn't want us, so I didn't want him!

Little did I know, he was going to assert, his control, the very next summer . . .

Cynthia.

Chapter 16

What do you mean, by his control? Well, I was placed on the train, in New London, Connecticut, in June of '75, for the ride to Penn Station, New York City. In Penn, I passed by the second homeless person, I'd ever seen, since London.

In the distance, I saw Maria, Trini, Melissa and Marisa, coming toward me. "Where's my father?" I asked. "He's parking the car," Maria said, "and if, you came here, to start any shit, between me and your father, I'll slap you down so fast! . . . You'll never even know . . . what hit you!"

I was disgusted and deeply hurt. I wanted to get on a train, straight back, to Connecticut. When Dad did show up, I just kissed him and said, "Hi Dad."

We all went to Westchester Country Club, to meet Maria's family, because her sister was a member. Dad, had thrown my suitcase, in the rear seat of the wagon and placed me there, also, at the back . . . and I watched him and his, "new family," up front.

I became ill; I vomited in my throat, at the sight and the betrayal, of it all. He opened the rear door and slapped me across the face, "Don't start your snot nosed shit . . . or I'll beat your ass, this is my new family, so behave yourself!"

I said nothing Soon, all Maria's relatives came to the car. I felt as though, I was in a nightmare awake . . . Everyone ignored me, even the twins. No one wanted me there, especially, my father. The purpose of my visit was, Dad insisted, I go with him to Alabama, to see his Mum, Gran, sister, Aunt Betty and her grown girls, Nancy Jo, Virginia and Laine . . . alone!

We left Westchester at midnight, to drop off Maria and girls, in Middletown Pennsylvania, or so I thought, I was told, but that was not to be, we only dropped off one twin, Marisa. When we started to leave for Alabama, the next day, I said "Dad, I thought just you and I were going to Gran's alone. He hit me so hard; I fell over, with my suitcase. "Shut your Goddamned mouth, mind your fucking business and stop your snot-nosed shit, before I beat your ass!"

Again, he put me and my bag, in the back of the station wagon and I had to watch him treat Maria and her girls, Trini and Melissa, like gold!" And me, like feces. I did not understand why . . . How could I? . . . at nearly sixteen.

Another aspect of the trip was, to get my Pennsylvania drivers license, on my sixteenth birthday, which would be July 28th, and drive the '68 Mustang, directly home to Connecticut and Mum. That became my beacon . . . the promise of my own license and car, to escape his hellish nightmare.

The two weeks in Alabama, were bizarre. Melissa, Trini and I were rented a room, at the Decatur Inn, near that infamous, flatbed accident river bridge. I was placed in charge of the money. Somehow, Dad remembered, he had taught me how, to handle it.

We visited Gran and family, only a couple of times. Mostly, we were three young girls, alone at the inn and we had to cross, a busy, bridge access road, to eat our meals?!? I was worried about hitting cars, as we crossed. I could never enjoy my food.

After two weeks, we piled into the station wagon, our respective assigned seats for the journey, straight through, back to Pennsylvania.

There were about three weeks left, until my 16th Birthday. How I longed to get out there! As we stopped, at various attractions or tourist points, I had to watch Dad, buy whatever Maria and her kids asked for, as he would buy me the cheapest trinket, he could find.

They were now, the recipients, of whatever, they desired and I was offered tokenism, to soothe his soul.

I couldn't believe that, a person could choose others, over their own child . . . yet . . . I was living it! Watching it! Suffering it! All I could recall was the speech he gave, when he took the job, at Three Mile Island, "I, haven't reached the wrung, on the ladder, I'm satisfied with yet! I'm going to build an empire, to leave you kids . . ."

The whole, entire reason, he said he wanted to build Three Mile Island, was for us! And now, he was frittering it away on strangers! The words of my Polish Great-Grandmother haunted me . . . "A bird doesn't shit in its own nest!" And he . . . had destroyed the nest. How unnatural. How could he actually go, on and on, forgetting . . . I was his child . . . not just some lump, who was tagging along!

When we reached Maria's house, a most strange lifestyle ensued. The dishes, were never washed, the bathroom never cleaned, the house was filthy and flies, were in abundance. As Dad and Maria, would go to work, at the Three Mile Island, by day, I would go to work, as Cinderella, for I could not take the squalor.

Melissa and I fought . . . every day. Soon, it came to her, kicking and pulling my hair and me trying, to diffuse it, I had enough! And called my mother, "Mum, please come get me, I can't stand it here, one more day!" She said, "I'll be there, in the morning, watch for me, tell no one . . . and be ready!"

She pulled up at approximately 11 a.m., with Nanna and Dziadzi. We went directly to a motel, in town and feared . . . all the while, Dad would find us . . . and do God knows what!?!

After a tense rest, we left the next day. The "Welcome to Connecticut," sign was the only thing, that finally calmed me. I decided at that very moment, Dad would have to make time and visits, for me alone, because I would never subject myself, to his slovenly existence and lousy treatment ever again! He would have to see me one on one, after all, he chose Maria and her kids, as his new life, but I did not.

Back in Connecticut, I was reunited with my relatives and all my friends. I was frustrated, that I had left before my drivers' license and without the Mustang, not knowing how that situation, would play out. In time, I got my Connecticut license and Dad did drop off, the Mustang, in Connecticut, at my brother's apartment, where he lived with his wife, Debby.

In the fall, I was driving to school every day. My love for Diane's brother, Dave, had grown over the summer, especially when I was in Pennsylvania. Thoughts of him and the fun we had, hanging out, driving around, when I spent nights, in Diane's room, for girlfriend sleep overs, kept me sane, through the ordeal in Pennsylvania.

How I longed, for Dave to view me as a girlfriend, rather than just a friend. That was never to be, because although we were super compatible, he had an impediment. I wasn't blonde, or drop dead gorgeous, nor did I have a perfect nose and perfect teeth. The one thing, he would have liked to do with me, would be have sex. That, I put off limits, although occasionally, he would indicate, that he would welcome a sexual relationship, only. Ha! Ha! I guess he was ahead of his time in 1975 . . . he wanted to invent friends, with benefits! I couldn't oblige him, my first love for him, was so deep, I knew sex, then rejection from him, would have destroyed me. I was truly afraid, of the power, it would have over me!

That fall, the eleventh grade began, upon my return, to the Norwich Free Academy and was a period, of adjustment. I had lost my virginity, in the spring of '75, to my first steady, a nice neighbor of Cheryl and family, named Phillip. We dated a few months and then I called it off, before I left, on the train, to see my father. I now had to pass by him in crowds. So much had changed, since that spring. Dave graduated, Diane transferred, to St. Bernard's High School, in Uncasville, due to the bullying.

I was driving and working, as a fitting room model, at John Meyer of Norwich, in the Emily M division, employed by my great aunt Mary, John's right arm. Now, Mary was my grandfather's sister and also, the sister to Father Walter and she had been the bookkeeper, of a men's pants factory in historic, downtown, Norwich, Connecticut.

Mary had separated with her husband, in the Catholic way, many years before and took vacations with quote, "the girls." It was my aunt Mary, who one day after a trip, with the girls, to an island, named Bermuda, in the early 1960's, showed John Meyer, her boss, the as she called them, "Bermuda Shorts!" she had bought there. She told him, "John, it's time to get into women's clothing, you'll never get ahead, with just men's pants!"

John Meyer, listened to her and they together, brought us, what she called, "Bermuda Shorts," in madras plaids, for women, although, in a men's cut, to the United States. From there John Meyer, listened further, to my aunt Mary. It was my aunt, who told him, "Madras handbags! To match the shorts, with wooden handles and then to slay, the entire women's wear market."

Before Dior, before Calvin Klein, there was John Meyer of Norwich, Emily M and a line of uniforms, named Omniform, for airline stewardesses and the professionals, all inspired by my aunt Mary, to her good friend, John Meyer. She had taken an obscure men's, small pant factory in Historic, Norwich, Connecticut and helped John build an empire! He later, sold his Jones Apparel Group. Mary and John are long gone, but Jones New York, still lives today! Aunt Mary, designed the once John Meyer logo, of Norwich, a tree, a family tree and from that tree, our family, in Connecticut and Rhode Island, still live well, off its graces . . . until this day! Truly, Mary was the women's apparel pioneer!

Life was getting so much better for me . . . or so I thought. Little did I know, the danger that was lurking, at Thanksgiving time.

Cynthia.

Chapter 17

Over the summer of 1975, Mum's alcohol consumption and its effects, became deadly. The week before Thanksgiving, she was in such ill health, that she began to vomit, urinate and defecate blood. She wasn't eating and was putting down a quart, of Old Grandad a day.

I called Billy. He came over with his wife, Debby and Nanna, for a family intervention. They all wanted her to go into the Norwich State Hospital, in Preston, Detox Unit. She broke down and begged them, not to commit her, that she'd try AA. I'll never forget, the moment, she made the call, for it was one of the best . . . in my lifetime. She said, "Hello, I'm scared, my name is Celene and I think I'm an alcoholic."

AA Central gave her, the name of a woman, Rita, to call and the rest. as they say . . . is history!

By the grace of God, she started her quest, on the road to recovery. I began to see a new woman, in Celene. I was getting a chance to experience her sober and working on her own character defects. An honesty and peace, we'd never known, came to dwell with us and she was able to cope with Dad and his bullying and remote control, effectively.

I met a new boyfriend, Steve, just before Christmas and Mum started dating a new acquaintance, named Gary. She took a job bookkeeping and attended daily AA meetings. God had heard my prayers . . . again, that were so desperate, before her recovery, "Dear God, please don't let Mummy die! Please, I beg of you, I love you, goodnight!"

Steve was a tall, dark, handsome guy. At school, we'd hold hands, kiss and cuddle and pass notes between classes. Our sex life, heated up and we were very happy! We had it all! Good jobs, plenty of cash, cars and goals, for the future! He, wanted to be a Doctor, I, wanted to be a lawyer. There was just one problem we had, a girl named Cathy, who had a mad crush, on him and did everything, to have me see her, with him as he met me, between classes.

This pattern, of school, working, Steve, Mums recovery and contentment, in general, followed me, nearly to graduation, from the Norwich Free Academy, in June of 1977. Of course, Dad was still stingy, with the money, an absentee father and brutal over the phone, but I had new coping skills, Mum had shared, from AA. Five weeks before graduation, I broke up with Steve. I'd had enough of Cathy, fawning over him and getting rides, to and from school, with him. Yet, the biggest issue was, his attitude! "I'm going to UCONN, in the fall, you're going to Mohegan. You will stay home nights, until I get home weekends!" became his constant speech.

Between his need for attention, from other girls and his, all too Greek, "I'm the man . . . I say what goes!" attitude, I made the break. I decided to enjoy the summer of '77 and let fate, take its own course. Because Dad had gifted Billy, with a brand new, Chevelle Malibu Convertible, when he graduated St. Bernard's High School, in 1972, I thought . . . the least he could do was the same gift . . . for me!

I asked for a new, Ford Mustang II Convertible and he kept me in suspense, up until Graduation Day! Since the family relationship, was almost non-existent, or at the least, severely strained, we all agreed to meet for lunch, at 1 p.m in the Picadelli, at Norwichtown Mall.

Mum and I arrived in the Mustang and met Dad, Billy and his wife, Debby, at a comfortable table. An episode, of the Twilight Zone . . . couldn't be more bizarre! There we were, pretending to be a close family, so Dad could save face, while in town! Anyone who knew us knew, he was shacking up, with the quote, "Other woman," in another state and Mum was dating locally!

They knew too, that Dad didn't want a divorce, after all that drama, of St. Patty's Day '74 . . . He would tell Maria, "Celene, won't give me a divorce!" but, he never asked for one . . . since that first day, he officially started, his affair odyssey. I was truly embarrassed at his hypocrisy, in the face of the local onlookers and in Norwich, Connecticut, where people, are very nosey and snooty.

When lunch was done, we decided to take in the Rose Garden, for photos. As we walked out of the mall, Dad pointed, to the first car in the row and handed me keys, saying, "There's your car, Sweetie!" I nearly flipped! In the spot, was a brand new, 1977, Triumph Spitfire, candy apple red and gleaming! I said, "Yeah . . . right Dad!"

"Your name is on it . . . it must be yours!" he quipped. I walked to the front and sure enough, it said, "Cindy," on a custom, vanity plate. "Thanks Mum! Thanks Dad!" I said; and hopped in. I needed to put Mum first, because it was from her too! Whether, he wanted to acknowledge that fact, or not! If she hadn't sent, the Military Police away, on several occasions, during our life, years before, he would have been Court-marshaled! She saved his naval career, on more than one occasion! She was never one, to recall that fact, but I was! I kept it . . . in reserve!

When I pulled into the Norwich Free Academy, parking lot, for the Commencement, all the clique, snooty, rich kids, jaws dropped! "Where did you get THAT CAR!?!" was repeated, over and over. So, on the last day, they all got to see, that I had as much, or more, than their rich parents, would GIVE . . . THEM! "My parents gave this to me, for my Graduation present." I repeated, over and over.

Suddenly . . . and fleetingly . . . I was accepted, by them, but I cared not! After Graduation, we dined at the Lighthouse Inn, New London, on lobster.

Dad left about 9 p.m. in the Mustang, to go back to . . . the other woman and Three Mile Island. I saw Mums whimsical, fantasy, of a reconciliation crushed . . . again! And . . . would see it, until the end. She was a hopeless romantic and Roman Catholic, to boot! Again, I had to comfort her, for several days, until she got back, into reality!

Gently, I would tell her, "Mum, he's never going to leave Maria, trust me, I know, I was with them, she's got some sort of hold, over him, maybe it's for the best, he was horrible to you!" That never soothed my Mother. She believed, in fairy tales and that one day, he would see the error, of his ways. She hoped and prayed, it would be before the end of his life, for his own soul's sake. For we reasoned as the Bible says, a man who commits adultery, forces his wife to commit adultery, therefore, both, are his sin, our Catholic Church doctrine, intact.

Wow! Summer! A great job, money to burn and Misquamicut Beach! With no ball and chain boyfriend! Awesome! I drove the Triumph, to Father Walter's cottage, every day. I'd go into work, in the morning, to try on the Emily M, samples and be a beachcomber, the rest of the day! Just me and my Spitfire! I'd break out the Hawaiian Tropic, number two and damn . . . I was looking gorgeous!

I had braces on my teeth, the latest hairstyle, a super wardrobe a dark tan and money in my pocket! I was a catch! Well . . . no one caught me. On July 28, 1977, I had my first legal drink, in the Village Greene Bar and Disco, in Norwich, Connecticut.

Life was good! Or, so I thought. The bar scene became my nightly hobby. Disco, was in her full bloom! What a time to be 18! We had Planned Parenthood, on the one hand and no AIDS, on the other hand. The kids in the sixties had, paved the way . . . but WE . . . had arrived!

One night, at the Greene, I saw a girl, from my last gym class, at Norwich Free Academy. The girl's name was Ingrid. We had a few drinks and reminisced, about the NFA showers, with the ladies, standing on the ladders, watching us and making sure, we washed our, "Pits and privates!"

I told her how, I got out of it, by saying . . . I had my period, a few weeks in a row and how they called me, in to, "monitor, my periods!" after that. Piss your pants funny!

She, introduced me to a nice guy, she was hung up on, Mike and his friend, Jeff. How could I know, ahead of time, what meeting Jeff, would do to me? Who could have warned me . . . would I have listened?!?

Cynthia.

Chapter 18

Jeff was the first guy, to take an interest in me, since Steve. I was lonely and starving, for affection. "I want to drive your car, tomorrow!" Jeff said. We set a time to meet. I was not too attracted, to his looks, so I wasn't going to show. At the last minute, I thought, "What the hell!" I arrived at his house, a bit late. He was glad; I came and hopped in my driver's seat. What started as buddies soon, turned physical and I began to smoke, all the pot, this dealer, would give me.

His mother was at home, dying of cancer and I helped, by working part time, answering the phone, for their family, appliance repair business. Jeff took my love, of music, to new heights. The time we spent together, was all about smoking weed, going out to clubs, him, performing "air guitar," for me . . . and passion.

He'd tell me, we would get married, in about a year, I never said yes or no, I just continued to party-on. I was grateful, that he insisted, I not, go with him, when he'd pick-up a pound of marijuana. He didn't want me to know them, or them, me. I respected his protection.

We had been going out, approximately a year, in October of 1978. Things were rocky, as he had another girl, Elise, on the side. What he didn't know . . . was, I also had a side lover, the son of Daddy's Jetport buddy, Bill . . . Bill junior. We had met at a cookout and he wanted to drive my car.

He proposed, "Friends, with benefits and I was all in favor. Bill was more gorgeous than Dave and as Dad pounded, into my head, when younger, before he left us, "Honey, when you marry, it's just as easy to love a rich boy . . . as it is to love a poor boy!" I didn't know, or care, if our affair, would ever lead to marriage! I used him; he used me, neither one cared.

A few days before Christmas, 1977, I was on the way to Jeff's house, when an old Rambler, plowed into the front of my Spitfire! The front end, was demolished, the windshield shattered and I ended up, between a telephone pole and a cement wall, with no room, to spare!

The only injury, was self-inflicted, as I dusted the crushed windshield, off my lap and crawled out, I sliced the side of my left pinkie. God had spared me. It didn't seem possible, looking at what was left, of the car. When Jeff, discovered my side, bed partner, he flipped out! I told him, he was no better.

The last night we spent together, would be a horror show! Mike took us and several, other potheads, out to party, in his sexed up, GMC Van. They passed a, "pin joint," and proudly displayed a Glad bag, of the pot. The buds looked like cockroaches, in a bag, all black, all uniform in shape. "This shit is African Black!" Jeff said.

As I drew off the pin joint, I thought my lungs, would explode, inside my chest! One hit, off that bone, sent me into orbit . . . The next day, Jeff's lung collapsed and I saw the X-Ray. When the doctor described, what had happened and just what a lung, looked like or didn't look like, on the shrilled up side, I vowed . . . to quit pot and cigarettes, that day!

Jeff spent several days, in the ward, with a tube in his chest, until the lung healed. I never saw him, when he went home. I was afraid to. I was dealing with my own, ill effects, from that marijuana.

I was tripping . . . the day after I smoked the African Black, was the first of approximately, forty days, of hell. A blood test, had indicated, that PCP, or Angel Dust, was in my body. The trips came and went, until my bloodstream cleared . . . the two worst ones . . . nearly killed me!

I woke up, in the middle of the night, the first night, after that van ride. It was dark in my room and I felt, as though my skin and organs were gone . . . and all I could feel, was my own . . . skeleton and my brain . . . seeming to be on fire! I ran to the bathroom, turned on the light and saw a most hideous sight!

My reflection was a sort of, a half-bull, half-demon head, with steam, pouring out of my nostrils! I'd shut my eyes, but the head would not disappear, until I'd slap my face, violently and come out of the illusion. I told no one about it. The only way I got help, was . . . a few days later, the Norwich Bulletin, had a lead story, about a foiled plot, to steal a submarine and take it out into the Atlantic Ocean, and point a Nuclear weapon, at the east coast!

This began a cycle of panic attacks, which would slam me, several times a day, I was afraid to look at another human and person, in print or on the television. I could barely be around my relatives! I feared the end of the world! And . . . nuclear war! My heart would pound, so fast and I would . . . hyperventilate, all at the same time! I thought I was going to die! . . . Over the forty days, in hell.

The last day, of an attack, from the Angel Dust, I drove to the Sacred Heart Church, for mass, in Norwichtown It was a 5 p.m. Saturday service. I was in the front row and the last . . . most intense . . . attack . . . hit me! Reciting the Apostles Creed, I began to cry and understood it all . . . for the first time! I had recited it, hundreds of times, in my life, but now, it was truly, I was knowing and feeling, its meaning. I started to cry, like a baby and shake in the pew, I had to get out of there . . . I drove the three mile trip, to our apartment, ran to my room, grabbed my Bible and prepared to die.

I took my pulse . . . it was 130 beats a minute; my heart was pounding, out of my chest, as I grasped for air! I opened to a page and my eyes fell on text which I began reciting . . . after several paragraphs, I snapped instantly, out of this panic-attack!

I was reciting, "Jobs, prayer, for death!" I didn't want to die, I wanted to live . . . and get better!

The next week, brought a new psychiatrist, into my life, named Dr. Parthenis. He was on staff, at the Norwich State Hospital, yet took private, evening appointments, with me. He was able to do, what Molly Brooks, a psychologist, of the Connecticut College, in the Quaker Hill, that I had visited, the year before, could not do.

When he listened to all my issues and woes, he would pose simple questions . . . designed to illicit simple, truthful answers. I came to know, that the forty days in the throws . . . of a PCP trip . . . were self-explanatory The science, proved it! The panic and anxiety attacks were, because I had; had, the "rude awakening," during the

PCP trips . . . the prayer for death, of Job, was death, of the life, I'd been leading . . . on the downward spiral.

Hence, as the Bible said, I had truly been, "Born Again!" Not as a Catholic, or a Christian, but as a human, who had to come to grips, with my own mortality . . . and life! On life's terms! And, on planet, Earth! A day of great change came, when Billy came to give me a, "pep talk,"

"Life is just . . . a series of goals," he said. "You must set one and meet it!" I agreed it would be, the best course of action.

I enrolled, in Huntington Institute, school of business, in Norwich, for office accounting. The term would begin, in January, of 1979 and last through September. I would become a bookkeeper, like Mum had done, in Business School. I began dating, a cute guy, named Kenny.

He was smitten with me and the '78 Datsun, Dad bought, to replace the Spitfire! Kenny was a charming, romantic guy, who's specialty was singing . . . just like Stephen Bishop! I was enthralled, with his sexuality and charisma. He had other women, on the side, but I did not care . . . as long as I could be his "main squeeze," it was okay, by me.

His big thing, was not pot at all . . . it was alcohol and being that I had sworn-off pot and cigarettes, since the Jeff days . . . Kenny was perfect! For me! Or so I thought! In the spring of 1980, I'd had ENOUGH . . . of his straying!

I had given up Bill, on the side and I wanted Kenny, to give all his side women. He would not. That, plus, our mass . . . alcohol consumption and the fact, that because of him . . . I had totaled my Datsun . . . on Laurel Hill in Norwich, with him as a passenger, breaking through the telephone pole, at the Laurel Tire Building and slamming, into the brick structure and luckily walking away . . . again . . . became enough of a sign, that this insane relationship and behavior, had to stop!

I took a job at the Thermos, Sun packer Cooler line, in April, of 1980. I worked first and second shift, alternately. I saved all my money, between my mattresses. I didn't date anymore, just concentrated on family and work. I got very sick of assembly line work and decided to quit.

Billy got me, a part-time job, in September, at Janie Schaeffer's, Professional Answering Service, in Norwich. There, I met a woman named Lee, who would come on, third shift, weekends. We bonded. In October, Lee said, "We need a proofreader, at the local newspaper. I want you to apply!"

I was open to the idea and hoping, it would help me change my life . . . for the better! What I didn't know . . . was just how it would!

                                                                  Cynthia.

Parents, William and Celene, courting, 1950

Mom, Billy and Me, home from the hospital, August 1959

Left to right Godfather Joseph, Mum, Me and Cousin Chester

Christmas, In Bonnie Scotland, 1966 and "The pram"

Camping and fishing, Loch Lomond, Scotland, April 1967

"Sammy, Salmon," Loch Lomond, Scotland, April 1967

Dad, Me and Billy at "Rest and be Thankful," Scotland, April 1967

"Onich," shore point, "Yanks," waving Simon Lake, out to sea, Early 1967

First Holy Communion, May 1967, On the grounds, "Onich," Toward by Dunoon, Scotland

Sand Beach, Toward by Dunoon, Scotland June 1967

Camping: Epping, Forest, London, England, July 1967

Tower Bridge, London, England, July 1967

Köln Cathedral, Köln, Germany, July 1967

Snow White and the 7 Dwarfs, Fountain, Köln, Germany, July 1967

Rudesheim, on the Rhine River, Cruise, Germany, July 1967

Kateberg, on the Rhine River, Cruise, Germany, July 1967

Koblenz to Mainz, return train trip,
of cruise, Germany July 1967

King Ludwig's Dream Castle, Germany, July 1967

Salzbergwerk, Berchtesgaden, Germany, "Salt Miners," July 1967

The Bridge of Sais, Venice, Italy, July 1967

A Fishing Village, near Pisa, Italy, July 1967

Atop the Leaning Tower of Pisa, Italy, July 1967

Enjoying the grounds. Leaning Tower of Pisa, Italy, July 1967

Victor Emanuelle Monument, Tomb of The
Unknown Soldier, Rome, Italy, July 1967

Inside The Colosseum, Rome, Italy, July 1967

St. Peter's Basilica, The Vatican, Rome, Italy, July 1967

Lugano Fountain, Lugano, Switzerland, July 1967

Aurnella, of Rome, Italy and Cindy's, eighth Birthdays', July 28, 1967 at camp, Lake Lugano, Switzerland

"The Pose," Swiss Miniature, Lugano, Switzerland, July 1967

Our Last stop: "Ice cream" post, touring, Europe, Eidenborough Castle, Eidenborough Scotland, July 1967

Playground, Westbay, Dunoon, Scotland, late Summer, 1967

Cynthia, again, Staring into the Sun on the grounds, "Onich," Toward, by Dunoon, Scotland, Fall 1967

Fruit tree enclosure and grounds, "Onich," Toward, by Dunoon, Scotland, Fall 1967

Chapter 19

On the day of my interview at the local newspaper, Lee greeted me and took me to meet the man; secretary to the Manager. I found him to be a likable, yet cantankerous and eccentric, individual. He was kind to me, and said, "If you want the job, it's yours, I trust Lee's judgment, don't disappoint me."

We went to the newsroom and passed into the office of the Manager. They left me there, for the interview with Mr. Cruikshank and the man who would be the Supervisor. They put me through all the interview paces, yet I knew, the job was mine, before I'd even met them.

Again, a job and money came easily to me . . . even fell in my lap . . . just as, the modeling and answering service had. I started the next day, it was in October of 1980 and fall was in full hue, around us. I enjoyed the ride into work and looked forward to a new and bright future.

I was sat at a desk, in a climate controlled, advertising production room and began the task, of reading, every display ad, to appear, in the next days newspaper. I had to check, for typographical errors, as well as visual production errors. Dad's speed reading course was, my saving grace. They were pleased, with my work.

Two of my five working days, were spent building display ads, in paste up, from which, I became very gifted, at doing. Those were the two days, a senior lady, named Terry, kept part time hours, to supplement her social security. I loved the paste up and camera work. I made me more astute, when the three proofreading days, came around.

Things, in the family realm were more peaceful. Billy and Debby had a baby son, named Billy the third, born that August and

Mum and I, always the best of friends, were content. Neither of us had men in our lives, so we had a lot of time together; by the grace of God, on the twenty third of October, marked five years of sobriety, for her, in AA.

In those years, she had weathered Dads pseudo-reconciliations and repeated betrayals, back to Maria, in addition, to the accident, at Three Mile Island, in early 1979 and his vow then, to return to the family, only to be drawn away, again, to a higher paying job, out in Utah. It was ironic, that he first moved there with intent, to finally get rid of Maria, yet . . . she joined him there, in Utah, shortly after his move.

I began to pity him. He didn't know who, or what he wanted anymore. Mum, just accepted it all. She truly lived her AA handle, Serene Celene. The New Year 1981 seemed so blessed, I could finally help Mum financially and we were both in good places emotionally. I was spending much of my time, with her parents, Nanna Stashia and Dziadzi. We were so compatible and they were such loving, giving, caring and supportive people.

I'd go to their house, on my lunch hour, from the local newspaper and along with them and Mum, we'd enjoy traditional Polish foods. I was so very content. I didn't need a man in my life. I had been on the journey, to recovery, in my own right, with Mum and AA . . . all was well.

Then there was the day, during Holy Week. Cheryl's son, Mark, was staying at Nanna's, because he was sick and his parents worked. I had my lunch and before returning to the Bulletin, I went upstairs, to use the bathroom. There, twelve year old Mark stood, brushing his teeth, crying and trembling. His body, especially his abdomen, was blown up, distorted; he looked pregnant, and filled with fluid!

I said, "Are you okay, Mark?!?" He broke down and I took him, into my arms. He told me how scared he was. As I held him, the God spoke to me, in a word of knowledge The words rolled off my lips, "Mark, you're very sick, it's going to take a very long time, but you will get better . . . " With that I kissed him and left him, at the sink.

I went directly back to the kitchen table, sat down and told Mum, Nanna and Dziadzi, "Mark has cancer; I don't know what kind, but its cancer!" Nanna scolded me, saying, "Don't even say that, Cinda Mae!" "I'm telling you . . . he has cancer!" I said firmly. It was time to go back to the Bulletin, so I left.

He was taken to the Backus Hospital, in Norwich and then, he was taken directly, to the Yale New Haven Hospital, in New Haven, Connecticut, diagnosis, cancer. Not any old cancer, oh no . . . but a very rare, Burkett's Lymphoma. The next day, his brain swelled, then the decision whether to tap it or not, fell into his parents lap.

A lady doctor, named McIntosh, was put in charge. The decision was made, not to tap and what ensued, was the hellish nightmare, of a sick, potentially dying child. I'll never forget that first night, at Yale New Haven Hospital. Cheryl clung, to our family and her husband, Harry, clung to his family, in another, separate room. I saw then, that their marriage was doomed.

All of 1981, until November, was about working and being there, for their younger daughter, Michelle, my Godchild. Cheryl and Harry, spent days and nights, in New Haven and Michelle, slept in my top bunk beds, at night, went to the school, by day and was passed around, among the relatives, for safe keeping.

I tried to be the best Godmother, in the world and give her some semblance, of a childhood, I knew would never be the same, due to Mark's illness and the impending demise, of their parents marriage. She became my cause, my mission. Mark fought the disease valiantly, through chemo, radiation and transfusions. His attitude was remarkable! Even to the point, of saying, "I don't have cancer!"

Everyone in the family was crushed, that he had to suffer, with the illness. We prayed and helped them with a wild abandon. Mark was the one, who needed all our strength, in addition, to his own and everyone from the youngest, to the oldest, in the family, delivered. Of course, I knew he would not die, from the first.

Bill, Jetport Bill Junior, came back into my life, briefly, during the summer of '81. We had drifted apart, from our, "friends with benefits," the summer before. This time was different for me; I began to think, "Why can't we pursue a meaningful relationship?" After a few meaningless nights, of bar flying and sex with him, I made the request just before, "Bill, this is all well and good, but I want more. I want to see more of you, more often, or I don't want to see you at all!"

In his conceited, arrogant way, he got up and said, "I can't believe you're saying this to ME! You're blowing me away, Uh! You're growing up on me!" With that, I had my answer. I got dressed and went to the door; he tried to persuade me to reconsider. I just said, "No, call me if you want . . . what I want, otherwise, goodbye and good luck!" I never got a call.

The Manager promoted me, to advertising services, in that fall. I was in the front office, with all the sales and support staff. I had walk-in display and customers and phone customers. The girls in the composing room, I had advanced from, were furious! "Who the hell was I?" . . . after only, nine months proofreading, to move up the ladder!?! A couple of them started, a nasty rumor, that I was having sex, with the Manager!

When the Manager heard it, he called the perpetrators, into the front office, told them it was false and if they wanted to keep their jobs, they needed to apologize, to me and stop the nonsense. They did and it was over. I was becoming lonely, for male company, in early October, yet, I refused to call Bill. Instead, I prayed, "Dear God, I'm thinking of joining a dating service, but I'm afraid, please tell me, if it is the right thing to do. I beg of you, I love you, goodnight."

Well, my form of prayer, had always been, my lifelong habit, always praying directly to God, always at bedtime and always waiting for his answers, as Mum had said, taught me, yes, no, or not now. A Thanksgiving time, the answer came. The fear had left me. I made an appointment, at Together Dating Service, in Mystic, Connecticut My mindset was "Okay God, if I don't meet the right man, I'll either stay home, with Mum, or go into the convent. You decide!" I met Doreen and laid out, my requirements. Could she fill them? Would she?

Cynthia.

Chapter 20

Downtown Mystic, was bustling, with Christmas shopping, in the center. I arrived in the evening and climbed the stairs, to the office above the Bee Bee's Dairy. Doreen greeted me with, "Welcome to Together!" The interview, consisted of approximately seventy five questions, the goal, was compatibility. A Photo was taken and she assured me, that for the next year, at a cost of $375.00, I would get a referral, a week. She showed me the sample. It was an NCR paper, with my name, typed to fit an envelope window and A mans' name, typed in a similar fashion, with each persons phone number, added.

It was up to the members, to call one another, talk on the phone and decide, whether to meet and date, or not. That concept, was strictly referral based, on the information, they would gather. My biggest priority, for a referral was, that the man not be a divorcee, or not have children, because a divorced man would not, be allowed to marry me, if the relationship turned serious, in my Roman Catholic Church and I did not, want to become, a stepmother.

As promised, my first referral came within a week. It was a man named David, who owned his own business, in Plainfield, Connecticut, making stainless steel exhaust systems, for classic cars, whose parts were out of production. He took me to New Haven, in a 1938 Dodge. We had dinner and saw Yellow Submarine, at an old movie theatre, bijou type. When we arrived back in Norwich, at my car, he kissed me and said goodbye. I never saw him again. We had nothing in common.

The weeks before Christmas, came another referral. A man named Gary, who was an engineer, at Milestone Nuclear Plant, in Waterford, Connecticut. We went out to lunch and then to his mobile home, to watch a, "Star Trek," movie, on his laser disc player.

I was so bored; I left before the movie ended. This date was more tedious, than the first!

I called Doreen, to ask why; I had only two referrals, in five weeks. She explained winter was a slow season, at Together, and, that she would give me, twenty six referrals, before the year membership, expired; she guaranteed it! Well, I was okay with that and I put dating, on the back burner, to focus again, on the family, especially, Mark and Michelle and work, at the local newspaper.

Christmas was joyful, yet somber, because Mark was bald and quite ill, from his course of cancer treatment. I couldn't help but wonder, what 1982, would throw our way, as a family, or me, as a member of Together.

On January 7th, Mum gave me my mail. There was a referral, for a man named, Alexander and I recognized the name, he had been my Biology Lab teacher, at the Norwich Free Academy, eight years earlier. I told Mum, "This guy is divorced; he was married to a girl, who was the sister, of my friend Cindy, who works at Two Legs, in the Norwichtown Mall. Now I'm pissed! Tomorrow, I'm going to let Doreen, have it!"

I crumbled the referral up and tossed it, in the garbage. I told Mum, "If this guy calls, I'll tell him, I'm insisting, on a replacement referral and he should do the same. I'll just tell him, no offense, I don't date, divorced guys and Doreen knows it!" Mum and I chuckled, at how weird, Together Dating Service was becoming!

The next evening, the phone rang "It's Alexander," Mum said I took the call and told him, what I had planned, to tell him. He took it well and the conversation ended. Three nights later, on the eleventh, he called and I answered. I told again, my speech about how Doreen, had made a mistake, by sending me a divorced mans, referral. He asked, if we could at least have a cocktail, together I saw no harm in that! I said, "Well, meet me, the bar near the office, at 9 p.m. next to the Norwich Bulletin.

Mum and I laughed, over one of his comments, when I had asked him, why he had called again, even though I gave him the divorced guy, brush off. His answer was, a hilarious, "Well, I was buying chicken breast, for my dinner and it made me think, to call you again!" It was awkward, meeting a former high school teacher for drinks, even though I was almost twenty three and he was almost thirty! I'd say, "Mister, I mean, Alex," during our cocktails and conversation.

I described just what, why; I had the no divorced guy rule. "The only way I could date you, Alex, without sex and not even getting serious, is if you were to apply, for an annulment, in the Catholic Church, from your first wife!" I told him, just before we said goodbye.

We had a great time, visiting at the bar and that's where I thought, it would end. The very next night, the phone rang, as Mum and I, sat down to dinner. It was Alex. He wanted to take me to dinner, on the upcoming weekend. "I got my annulment application," he said. He admitted, it would be good, for him to do, no matter whom he dated! I guess my preaching, worked.

That weekend, he took me for the full course meal, at the Bootlegger Restaurant, on the picturesque, Thames River, in Groton, Connecticut, just behind the historic, one time ship that was moored, named, Croaker, submarine. We dined, at January sunset and enjoyed nightcaps, in the lounge, afterward. Alex was a waiter there, several nights a week, to supplement his teaching salary . . . and the staff gave us, the royal treatment!

He began to tell me that night, about his love, of fishing and that he would be starting up for the season, in his Ranger Bass Boat, as soon as the law allowed, regarding opening day. Like life, he had the same zest, for his own life, as he displayed, all those years earlier, in the classroom. I began to find his consistent personality, after having studied him and all the other teachers, in the past, most endearing.

He was most sincere and wanting to make, a new life for himself, perhaps because thirty was, closing in. He chose the following weekend, to introduce me to his parents. He had met Mum, the night of the Bootlegger dinner and she thought; he was super! "My father, looks like me and he is like Archie Bunker," he said. He had no forewarning for me, about the mother.

Well, upon entering the parents' home, I was invited into the parlor, to sit. The father, Al senior, was a very nice, jovial guy. The mother, Eleanor, was still, deep and was totally sizing me up! She made it clear, she could be an adversary, but I thought, "Piece of cake! No one can beat Dad!" or so I thought . . .

When Valentine's Day came, I decided, to tell Alex, I could be falling, in love with him. I placed a three inch, classified display ad, in the local newspaper, stating simply, "Alex, I Love You, Cindy." Just after lunch, the FTD florist, delivered the Valentine Bouquet, to my desk, with a card, saying, "Happy Valentine's Day, Love, Alex."

Things were going very well between us. We were getting closer and we were happy. We were looking forward, to his annulment and a proper engagement. He invited me, to a homecoming party, at his sister, Cheryl's house, in Salem, for the first day of spring. Cheryl and her husband, Jeff, had just spent his post-navy employment time, for a few months, at his parents' home, in Ocean Reef, in the Key West, Florida. I was looking forward, to meet a woman, just one year older, than Alex and perhaps, equally as nice! How could I possibly know, how she would greet me? What she would say? And, how she would view me?

Cynthia.

Chapter 21

We arrived, before Alex's parents did. Soon, they came in, with the two other full grown siblings, a brother Tom and then, a brother Tim. The brothers were younger than Alex. One was three years younger, that was Tom and Tim was five years younger. The brothers and the sister, barely acknowledged, my existence.

I struck up a conversation with the brother-in-law, Jeff. "Did you go to Annapolis?" I queried. He explained that he had graduated, Annapolis and was in the nuclear program. I mentioned my Dad's naval career and Three Mile Island; he was interested, in my conversation. I kept it to myself, but wondered.. why he didn't finish, the twenty years, for navy retirement?

By the looks of the opulent home and antique heirlooms, I knew, he must have come, from wealthy parents. I knew that was not the case, with the wife, Cheryl. Cheryl was very rough around the edges and took control, of all those in attendance, except for me. I was a lady, yet, I held my ground, in not letting her, un-nerve me, with her sarcasm, overbearing, control freak, ruler of the family, mannerisms which were painfully, evident.

She had been gone, a while and I watched everyone, report to her and take her criticisms. She was rude, obnoxious and conceited . . . and I could find no reason, why she should think, the world, revolved around her and her whims. I knew instantly, by watching her, manipulate her husband and nuclear family, that she would eventually, try it with me. I could see, she was an out-of-control, overgrown, injured adolescent. I knew, to beware of her! . . . Far reaching tentacles!

I was never so glad, to leave a new acquaintances presence, as I was to leave hers! I had a chance to observe the, "still water-runs deep, mother!" and her boorish daughter. I hoped to keep my distance, from such toxic people, as my father . . . but would I be able to? I did not know.

Then there was Alex, who had such a good heart and nature! I thought surely, he was adopted, for he was not like any, of the negatives, I saw in his parents and siblings. I took everyone, at face value. I decided to interact, accordingly.

When spring was in full bloom, we boarded the Ranger Bass Boat, on Gardner's Lake, in Salem, Connecticut This was to be the first, of many fishing trips, to come. I loved to fish! Dad, Billy and I, used to get sandworms and take our gear, to the lower Submarine Base, in New London-Groton, Connecticut, to fish for flounder, next to the docked submarines.

Many a time, we'd fill a galvanized garbage can, to the brim! And, Dad would stand for hours, filleting them, for us, the family and our neighbors. I relished the good memories of Dad, I tried, to erase, the bad ones, or at least cope, as an adult, who had been through great counseling!

Alex brought my love, of the sport, back into my life. Occasionally, we'd go into the Thames River, at Dock Road in Montville, Connecticut and just cruise, up to the Norwich Harbor, at the back of the mouth, of the river, to New London Ledge, Lighthouse, we would return, before going back to bring the trailer, 'em, for the pickup of the boat.

Now Alex worked, when the summers arrived, for TVCCA, in Jewett City, Connecticut He was placed in charge, of a teenage crew of young men, who did clean-up projects, for municipalities. We got a good indication, from the Catholic Church, that his annulment would be swift, due to the duration, of their marriage, three and a half months, with no children and she had left, because, "I don't want to be married, anymore!"

With hope in our hearts, Alex bought me a promise ring, of engagement. He presented it to me, on my twenty third birthday July 28, 1982. I had picked it out, but didn't start to wear it, until then. We stopped by his parents' house, to make our intentions known. If looks could kill, I would have been murdered, by Eleanor's eyes. Al senior, on the other hand, seemed relieved, someone would take on his now, thirty year old, number one son!

The Annulment came through, in October, that year. I now felt freer to be with Alex. The impediment was removed! I kept residence at Mum's apartment and kept paying, one fourth of my take-home pay in room and board, yet, set up "camp," in his apartment.

We were so happy and planning our marriage and future. We spent more time, with both of our families and Cheryl and Eleanor, began to assert their control on our engagement. I couldn't make a move, positive, negative or indifferent, without them making cutting, hurtful, snide remarks, when Alex was out of earshot. I told myself, "Calm down, be a lady, consider the sources, you'll be his wife soon and it will stop."

We married, at St. Mary's Church, in Greeneville, Connecticut, on April 23, 1983. It was six months, of marriage preparation classes, covering all pre-cana issues that took us, to that happy day! My Great Uncle, Father Walter, the Misquamicut Beachcomber, came in special, from Kansas City, Missouri, to perform the ceremony. The happiest day of my life, was also the most stressful, up until that point.

Dad had been playing, reconciliation cat-and-mouse, with Mum, for over nine years, at that point. Every time, he tried to return to Mum, it ended! He'd go back and we would see that, he was going back to Maria! And he would say, over and over, "Oh! I have to go! Maria would be crushed!"

Well, Mum grew to expect all the reunions, as false hope. As I put on my simple wedding gown and veil, I was happy, yet hurt, because Dad had ruined the first wedding plans, he agreed to. It was so very cruel, at the time of the annulment; Dad had agreed to pay for everything, for my future nuptials. I went to the Allyn's Bridal Shoppe, in Downtown, Norwich, Connecticut, and picked out a $1,500.00, circa 1905 style wedding gown, complete with hat and parasol.

The officers club, at the Subase, New London-Groton, Connecticut was booked, for April in 1983. Things were moving along fine, 'til the invitations were to be printed. At eight weeks prior, Dad insisted, Maria be mentioned on them . . . I was floored! He was still married to Mum . . . had attempted umpteen phony reconciliations . . . and now . . . had the gall . . . to expect we bear further hurt and humiliation, as a family? By including her, on the invitation? As what? "William and mistress?!?"

As I stood in the mirror, looking at the stress boil, on my forehead, in my substitute wedding gown, the morning of my wedding, I further recalled, that everything had changed, when I said, "No! Maria can't be a part of my wedding day! I would not be happy, on my special day!"

Dad could care less, about me and my happiness, but I already knew that! He refused, to come, or to pay, without her. So there I stood, in that mirror, the morning of my wedding, about to leave for the marriage ceremony. I looked at the hundred dollar plain-Jane dress, I had to switch to! How I longed for my first choice. I was scared, whether Dad, would have the nerve, to show up! I had convinced Mum, that if he did, she would need a sheriff handy, to serve him divorce papers, before the ceremony, because . . . cutting me off . . . for the wedding . . . would most definitely lead to cutting her off, financially.

We didn't know, how the new, economy-style wedding, she, Alex and I, were now paying for, would go. We had done our best to pay for, "simple elegance." As I took one last look, in the mirror, I dreaded if Dad and Maria, would show and all of Alex's nuclear family, because they were, at least as mean, or meaner, than Dad!

Those issues bothered me, more than the appearance factor, or the change of reception location, or the change, from a live band to a DJ. So many dark clouds! So much change . . . on what was supposed to be, a happy day. Alex and I, had a lot of vipers, surrounding us, yet, we vowed to wed and be happy.

Would anyone affect that happiness? How could we possibly know?

Cynthia.

Chapter 22

The years between 1983 and my thirty second birthday, July 28, 1991, were spent coping, with my cruel in-laws, and my husband, allowing them to be cruel, to me. Also, many changes, in my family, were taking place and I did a lot of letter writing, to my Dad, he never responded.

Two of my closest relatives died during these years. Mum's parents, who were my rocks of Gibraltar Dziadzi, Stanley in 1988 and Nanna, Stashia in 1990. I had to watch it all and be by the grass-widow, Mum's side and go through all, the five stages, of grief; anger, denial, bargaining, depression and then, finally . . . blissful acceptance . . . along with disseminating their belongings, property and home. These things are very, painful and I know, but each of us has death, which is truly as natural as birth . . . to contend with.

Life was on a bizarre, status quo, just moving, at a snail's pace, in a limbo of feeling unloved and unfulfilled, for me. First, by Dad . . . all my life . . . and then . . . by my husband . . . for all my marriage. Another, very shitty, cruel phone call came in, from Alex's Mum, on that day, my thirty second birthday in 1991.

Over the course of the next few hours, in the screen house, at the back of the yard, over the patio, I told my mother, what I had told no one, in the days, weeks, months and years, until she died . . . in 1994. She came to know, that day, all that I had hidden. I had hidden it all, from her and my grandparents, even my best friend, Diane.

My husband and his family were very cruel and demeaning to me and became too much to bear, over the years, from '83, until that fateful birthday, the 32nd birthday, in 1991. To go into too much detail, will be too painful and rise too many hurt feelings, within me. To recap as briefly as possible, is as follows . . .

I never fully understood why Alex's first marriage failed, until, he finally admitted, his family did the same, to his first wife, that day, in the screen house, he admitted it, to me and to my Mother . . . Just, how they had all treated her, no wonder! She quote, "didn't want to be married, anymore!" Being married, to this man and into that family, became dreadful and heartbreaking!

My husband loved his family and their money. Whether they had a lot, or not, I don't know, but that was the case. They were his first priority. Some of the things I had to endure, for no good reason, were . . . the fact, that they and their money, where his first love, he hated his job, teaching teenagers and drank himself, into drunken stupors, every night.

Everything we did, revolved around him and his needs, because in his mind, "he took care of me . . . financially . . . so I should just, put up with them, all" . . . He'd say, "You're stuck with me pal, for better or worse!" The better, was his non-insistence that I not, work outside the home . . . and the things money could buy me. After all, of course, all his needs and desires, were met!

His family would treat me, so cruelly and he allowed it and they made, hurtful cutting remarks. They were trying to drive me away, just as they had done, the first wife! They'd refer to me in person as, "You're only chapter two! You don't work, you're too sensitive, you can't even make a mortgage payment, you don't give us a grandchild, you need to earn your keep, you should at least do all the dishes, over here on Sundays!" Ugh!

And those Sundays . . . sheer hell, sheer torture! At his parents' house, we'd all gather, nine adults and then, two grandchildren, the children of Cheryl and Jeff, two boys. Everything revolved, around the grandchildren and my mother-in-law's whims! She would insist, we all concentrate, on her two grandsons and then drag her feet, preparing a Sunday meal, which would not be seated, until she was nearly ready, to allow, those of us going back home, to go! Many a Sunday, we ate past 8 p.m.

She used the grandchildren and the food, to assert her control, over everyone's Sunday schedules. She didn't care, if you had other plans, she didn't care, if you had to work, the next day. She and her daughter's, selfish whims, were all that mattered. Every Sunday, from April '83, until that July in 1991, I would come home, driving the car, because I did not drink, the alcohol and my husband did.

And I would be crying, to him, on the way home, to my husband and begging him, to tell them, to stop their cruelty, to me. He was always so drunk. They all drank, even the mother of the children, even while pregnant, with them. I couldn't believe the amount, of drinking, except . . . the mother did not.

It was extremely hard drinking, being of Russian decent, it was something that they did, it was their culture. Well, my husband would ignore, my pleas, in the car. Instead, he'd ask me, "When's this shit gonna end?" I'd cry and beg, "When you end it! I did nothing to those people, I'm nice to everyone there and they hate me, for no good reason! I'm not married to them, I'm married to you and they don't, have the right, to be cruel to me!"

All this fell on Alex's deaf ears. So, on that day, in the screen house, on my 32nd Birthday and with my mother, now knowing, the things that I had been through, she asked him the question, "What did my daughter; do over there, to deserve their cruelty?" And, of course, he said, "Nothing."

I was ready to divorce him at that point, all things considered. I went through, the house and made lists, of who would get what, but sadly, oddly, I still, loved and wanted to be with him, if only he would finally be my husband! I waited, 8 long years, for him to do the right things by me, his wife. I stayed away from his family, at that point and he stayed with me. It was very stressful, although, I think he stayed just with me, I can never really be sure, he did not go over alone, for visits to co-bash, or co-trash me.

I never knew. I tried to think he didn't. I told him on Christmas Day, of 1991, when his parents didn't even, send us a return Christmas card, I said, "Alex, mark my words, someone, is going to get sick over there, their problem, your families problem is, they're so high and mighty, they're so, ah, superior attitude and they think that money is everything and they don't know, what a problem is yet! God, is sending cancer, to someone, and mark my words; again, they will call you then. Then and only then, will we be good enough, to come back, into their presence and perhaps be treated correctly!"

Well, in the early spring, of 1992, the unmarried brother, Tom, called to say, that . . . their mother, Eleanor, was dying, of female cancer and had less than 6 months to live! I took the call. When Alex came home, I said, "Sit down, have a drink, your brother called here today." I laid down what had been told, to me. I said, "Tomorrow, I will send Eleanor, one dozen, long stemmed, red roses, to the Backus Hospital, in Norwich, Connecticut. Alex, meet me out front, after school and we'll go in and we'll visit her, together and all will be well."

Shocked, he agreed and for the next thirty months, not six months, we watched Eleanor, rot away, from the reaches of the cancers that, consumed her entire body. The sister, Cheryl, would come in and out, from the Chicago area, by this time, but it was myself, Alex, his father and the two local brothers, that were here for her, in her final analysis, her final trial and her purification, by the God.

We left for Disneyworld, Florida, which we offered to cancel, because she was . . . touch and go. The day we flew back into Connecticut, it was in early August, of 1994. We went straight to the Backus Hospital. Eleanor was just about conscious, at that point and in a private room, as per Doctor Slater's, request. It was a death room, ladies and gentlemen. That's all I can say . . . on that!

When she saw me, she said, "How was your trip?" very weakly. "Move closer, I need to see you, you are beautiful Cinda Mae, your face, your teeth, your smile." Then she fell into a morphine sleep. While we were in Florida, the sister, Cheryl, had come in from Illinois and insisted, that a feeding tube, be put in, to placate her own self. That was something even Eleanor never wanted and yet, with no living will, any family member, can request force-feeding!

When we visited her sick bed, two days before she died, she was totally unconscious. As Eleanor lie there, I saw my husband well up with tears. I reminded him, of her no feed, no force feed wish and told him, that he should remind the father. That afternoon, he did and the next day, Al senior, had the gumption, to have it removed.

Eleanor died, August 10, 1994, approximately twenty four hours, after the feeding tube, was removed. She had outlived, her original death sentence, by two painful, cancer laden years, beyond the six months. The funeral arrangements were made and the witch, Cheryl, her daughter, as her own family called her, not my adjective, theirs! Flew in from Chicago, on her broom, as usual!

The day of the wake, was, of course, very sad, for those who deeply loved Eleanor. I was placed at the end, of the huge receiving line and that was fine, but of all those, who attended the wake and funeral, a few dozen people, either scoffed at me, gave me dirty looks, or completely ignored me, just as they greeted Alex! Standing directly next to me!

Eleanor was well liked and had held various, school, secretarial jobs, in the Montville Public School System, here in Connecticut, through the years, so ironic just like my Dad, or my husband, at work, she was at her best! At home, well, she was mean, controlling, vindictive and hypocritical, even to her own husband. He bore the brunt of her ire, as well as I did!

Al senior and I, were the two that bore her ire. Some of the same people, who were, rude to me, who didn't even know me, knew all her dirt and complaints . . . about me! Funny, these same people were trashed by Eleanor, or gossiped about by Eleanor, in my presence, at her own house! Over . . . the years.

If there's one thing I live by, it is, "Don't be a hypocrite!" But, as Dad taught us, "If someone is saying, or doing, bad things, about you or to you, it just means, they're leaving someone else alone!" I had to adapt that as my mantra, to be able to cope. All funerals are sad, yet this one was very difficult, for me to endure, because the hatred that she had begotten toward me was . . . all around me!

As a huge brood of vipers now, at the graveside, the undertaker announced, "Eleanor's family, invites everyone, to Peter's Restaurant, in Uncasville. No sooner, had he uttered those words and the sister, Cheryl, blurted out, "Ah . . . the Peter's Restaurant is only for close family and friends!" I have never, witnessed such an uncouth, mean, public comment. Who was to know, if they fit the description?!?

My mother asked Cheryl, "Are myself and my relatives invited?" Cheryl said, "No! There isn't enough room, for you and your relatives!" This was so insulting to my Mum, my Godfather and his wife and my great aunt, Mary. Now, they saw, that family clearly. I had to sit, through the worst meal of my life, watching all their chosen favorite, mean people, dining.

I was ashamed, my family was turned away.

Cynthia.

Chapter 23

Life, as strange as it is, had something totally devastating, in store for me. Soon after Eleanor was buried, Mum, Alex and I went to North Conway, New Hampshire, the two days, after the funeral, for a five night stay visiting Billy's three children, his ex-wife Debby and her second husband, Mark. The days and nights in New Hampshire, were great fun! As I swam in the pool, at the Sheraton Four Points Inn, in downtown, North Conway, New Hampshire, with the kids, I had to explain, the huge bruises, on my left arm, upper arm, inflicted by my sister-in-law, Cheryl, the day after, Eleanor, was buried.

It came about this way . . . Alex and I, called the father's house, that day, ah, after his mother was buried . . . in the morning. His younger brother, Tim, answered and said, "Cheryl and her family had left . . . to go back to Chicago."

So, we decided to go and spend some time with his father that day. So, at about 1 p.m., ah, we decided to go, we did not feel, that the father needed to be alone, for too long. We wanted to visit him, to comfort him. Imagine my surprise, when we entered that house and only the grandchildren, Al senior and THE SISTER, Cheryl and the younger brother's wife, Kim, were there!

The lie, over the phone, that they had all left, to go back Chicago, was designed, to entrap us! Over the course of about an hour, Cheryl and Kim verbally abused me, inside the den, with the father and the grandkids, in another part of the house. My husband was at my side and I could hardly believe, what Cheryl was saying.

She accused me of being the reason, her mother, had died from cancer. Alex, then found the strength, I don't know where, to debunk, her bologna speech. He then asked her . . . point blank, if all I had told him, over the years, of their verbal abuse, by verbal sledgehammers . . . if I had in fact, told the truth, at how they would destroy me, with their mouths, when he was out of earshot?

Well, his sister Cheryl was only, too glad and too indignant and responded, "Yes, we did say and do, all those things to Cindy!" She, in her grief and utter bizarre mindset, that I had somehow . . . killed their mother . . . finally, validated all the cruelties that I had endured, from 1983, to then, August of 1994.

When we got up to leave, Cheryl grabbed my left upper arm, not wanting us to go, screaming, "You bitch! You no good bitch, you yippy, yenta, bitched voice, bitch! Get back here! I'm not done with you yet!" I broke free and headed, to the back door. Again, she grabbed the same arm, in the same place, "I'm not done with you yet, bitch! Get back here, you killed my mother!" She nearly took my left arm out of its socket! I swear, if she'd have had a gun, she would have shot me dead, on the spot!

By this time, the three grandchildren, there was a little baby grand daughter now, that was from Kim and Tim, those children, were all abuzz around the scene, that Cheryl was making and I just, turned and said, to Cheryl, "'Em, it was one thing to abuse me, yet again, in the den, for no good reason and now, you are doing it, in front of the children! Think, of what you are doing and how, it will affect them! You need to stop this insanity, right now!" Still, she tugged me, back into the house!

Alex, finally, had to step in between, to break her grasp! My parting words were, "You have two sons, don't do to them and their girlfriends or wives, what you and your Mum, have done to me, all these years . . . I warn you, they will remember this day, do not make the same mistakes, with them, or you will lose them, please believe me!" Finally, free of it, we went directly, to the Montville Police Station, to report her assault.

The police accompanied us, back to the house. They told us to wait in the car, they would go investigate. Imagine, my horror and disgust and rejection and utter injustice, I felt, at what they told me, when they came back out. "Yes, Cynthia, you were assaulted by Cheryl, but . . . if you want to press charges, you will be arrested too!" "What!?!" I said. I explained the phone lie, setup, to get us over there;

they cared not and went on to say, "Al senior will, have you arrested, for trespassing, if you arrest his daughter, end of discussion!"

Well, my heart, my life, my once respect for the man, died that day. I said, "You mean to tell me, we were brought in, under false pretenses, that she was on her way, back to Chicago and then, she assaulted and abused me, after the father, let us, into the house and now he, to cover her crime, will say, that I've trespassed, to save her, from what she has done, to me!?!" The officer reiterated, "Yes! He will press charges, if you press charges, you both will be arrested!"

I thought, a moment and said, "Oh no! I won't! It's not fair, but what will I do? . . . No, I won't." Well, Alex and I decided, we sadly, needed to go into the, stay away, from the father mode, now also! This went on, for several months and then slowly, Alex asked, if I would forgive his father. I agreed, only because, the man was a pitiful alcoholic, missing, a mean, controlling, wife, WHY . . . I never knew . . . He didn't have to put up, with her cruelty, anymore, but, love is strange, as Dziadzi would say, "Love, what a disease and some people are sicker, than others!"

But, love, being deaf, dumb and blind, as it can be, as I said, I know, 'em, why . . . and he had a daughter, who had caused yet more, duress, in the family, then she just sashayed her way, back to Chicago, leaving her own Dad, alone, to deal with her own selfish aftermath and its consequences! Well, we picked up the beachcomber, my priest, Grand Uncle, Father Walter, on a Sunday; in August . . . it was a few days after, this whole incident, with Cheryl, assaulting me and us, coming back from North Conway, New Hampshire. Mum drove, to the Providence airport, so, myself and Alex and my Great Aunt Mary, 'em, went to pick up the priest, Father Walter,

the uncle.

Well, on August the 25th of 1994, Mum had her usual, Thursday night soirée, to meet her good friend, Norris, for grinders and a cruise, from Spicer's Dock, at Stonington, into the Fishers Island Sound. That night, at 9:30 p.m., she called me, to say she was back, in her apartment. Cool! Another grinder, dinner cruise, with Norris . . . complete!

Well at 10 p.m., the phone rang. I heard the panting, wheezing, not able to breathe person, on the other end. It was Mum. We had a plan in place, always, that in the event, of yet another asthma attack, she would call 911 and I would meet her, at the Backus Hospital ER. After about three minutes, of listening to her struggle and gasp, in between . . . the gasps, with long pauses and gulps of air, she said, "Cindy, I called 911, meet me at the ER."

I rose Alex out of bed and told him, "Mums having an asthma attack, we need to go, to the Backus ER, now!" We got our clothes on and got into the car, when we drove, down Kimball Road, onto Route 169, a tractor trailer truck was jackknifed, on 169, forcing us onto the back roads, through Occum, Connecticut, to the Backus ER. When we arrived, Mum was not there.

Along the way, over the Shetucket River, I said, "Dear God, please don't take Mum, please . . . I beg of you, I love you!" Norris had been called, before we had left, the house and would meet us, at the ER. Well, on the Old Canterbury Turnpike, past Occum, as I said my prayer, over and over, for God not to take Mum . . . I FELT my Mum and the Jesus Christ, come into the back seat of the car!

I did not see them, I FELT their presence. My prayer immediately switched to, "Okay, God . . . if you're going to take her, please don't make her, stay here and suffer, one heartbeat longer, than she has to!" I FELT their presence, until we rounded the curves, to the ER entrance. No ambulance, had delivered her yet. Norris and Alex, agreed to stay and await, her arrival, via the American Ambulance Company, owned by Ron Aliano, of Norwich, as I took the quickest route, through the Mohegan Park, to get to her . . .

Well, back at the apartment, I let myself in. There, was a scene, from Rescue 911! Okay, I told myself, she's on her way to Backus! Then, her neighbor next door arrived and rang the doorbell.

Cynthia.

Chapter 24

Now this neighbor, named Mary, of all things, was totally avoiding me and Mum, for about one year, prior to this incident. Why? I still don't know, until this day. She had a withered hand and seemed to have traces, of cerebral palsy, or multiple sclerosis, we did not know. Mary laid out, the Ambulance scenario, for me. The American Ambulance, of Norwich, Connecticut, had responded, to Mums 911 call.

Mary said, that when she was on the stretcher, she was moving, still alive and made eye contact, with Mary, who went on over, to the front door, to view all that was happening. She told me, "Your Mum was alive, on the way to the Ambulance; she looked directly at me, Cindy!"

Well, en route, over the city roads of Norwich, Connecticut, to the William Backus Hospital, my Mum died. I sped as fast as I could, not knowing that fact and arrived, at the ER entrance, where Alex and Norris, greeted me. I said, "Is she here yet!?!" Norris spoke, "Yes, and it doesn't look good, Honey!"

The three of us, were ushered into, an inner sanctum, private family room. Soon, an ER nurse said to me, "It's not good! You need to wait here, is there anything, you want me to tell, your Mum?" I reached into my handy-dandy, Dooney Bourke purse and produced, a brown scapular medal, of the Catholic Rite, of Our Lady of Mount Carmel; and asked, "Please, put this, on my Mums neck and tell her it's from her daughter, Cynthia and that, she loves her very much!"

With that, the nurse left. Within twenty minutes, Father Joseph Tito, of the Cathedral, of St. Patrick, arrived in the family room. Father Tito knew me well, he said, "Cindy, your Mother has gone,

God has called her home, now you must be prepared and do what you can do, to usher her, into the next realm, of eternal life!"

Soon, the MD arrived, saying, "'Em, that they would need to, clean Mum up, for a viewing, so to please, wait here and then, we will take you to her body!" I knew Mums prayers, had been answered and as . . . far be it from me, to block them, in any way, or to buck, her prayers. She had been preparing me, all my life, for her possible, untimely, death, due to asthma! . . . And now, it had finally arrived! It happened. I could hear her, echoing, from a little, tiny, girl, "Cindy, I'm asking God, not to take me, until you, are strong enough, to handle it!" As her refrain, reverberated over and over, in my mind! Who was I then . . . to question, the God?!?

Well, with that, I called Grand Uncle, Father Walter, at the Misquamicut family beach cottage, homestead, right after they told me, Mum was dead and I said, "Father, Mum is dead of asthma." He told me to, "Sit tight, keep my wits about me and that he and Great Aunt, Mary, would soon arrive!" Now, we're talking, in the wee hours, of the morning, perhaps, by this time, 'Em . . . 1 a.m. I said, "Father, Raymond and Jane, cousins, have opened their house and home, to us, with waiting arms, for us, to come. I will be waiting for you, there."

The rest of that night and into the wee hours, of the morning, we congregated at my cousin, Raymond and Jane's house. Father Walter, comforted me, like no one else, could! The Creator had sent him in, just four days prior, to Mums death. The Creator knew, only, HE, could console me, during the darkest days of my life, my sunshine . . . as she had sung to me, had been extinguished. What lie ahead, of me, without Mum, was certainly dismal . . . and grey . . .

My brother, Billy, tried to pretend, he cared about Mum, about me and I let him! Far be it from me, to, "Shit, in my own nest!" and let all comers, to the wake and funeral, know, just the truth, of his toxic relationship, to Mum!" He and I, could care less, about each other, but Mum? I vowed . . . her dignity and memory . . . would remain intact!

Approximately, 650 people came in and out, for the viewing, over the course of, 'Em, a day, day and a half. I had to have, the funeral mass, at St. Patrick's Cathedral, Norwich, Connecticut, to accommodate, the throngs . . . and they did come . . . out, even on the 30th, of August, on a hot summers day, yet with a monsoon rain, like you hadn't seen in years! They all came, to pay their respects.

We had four priests, concelebrating the mass, after the casket was placed, directly to my left, at the front right row, where I sat . . . after the homily, I arose, to speak, what I said, in love and tribute, to my Mum. When I was done, all were awestruck! Not knowing to clap, or continue! No one knew what to do, as they looked at me, after I spoke. In dignity and reverence, they continued, in the Catholic Rite, of Christian Burial, mass.

When the mass ended and we proceeded, down the long Cathedral aisle, toward the door, the monsoon intensifies even more! Whether one had an umbrella, or not, it did not matter! We were all, soaking wet, in our own clothes, in limousines, or cars, all the way, to Mums burial plot. At the plot, the rain did not subside. All the hearty, lovin', souls, who knew and loved Mum, stayed the course, all the way, to the cemetery.

I arranged for three hundred, or so, to dine at lunch, in the Knights of Columbus Hall, in Norwichtown. About 250 of the 600 or so, in the Cathedral, stayed all the way, through the funeral mass, the burial plot and the luncheon. For weeks, I had people calling, to check up on me. Dozens wanted my, "Ode to Mother," which I had compiled, especially, for her funeral mass.

Cynthia.

Chapter 25

And now, I'd like to share with you, I need to share with you, 'Em some information, which I feel, totally and completely. I want to share it with you . . . friend, whoever you are, wherever you are, because I care and I know, of what I'm speaking. No one can, prepare another person, for the death, of a loved one. Yes, my maternal grandparents deaths, in 1988 and 1990, respectively, were hard and sad . . . but Mums death . . . was the darkest, as I said, day of my life! That far!

She had, as I told you, prayed all her life, as a Mother, not to outlive, myself or Billy, nor to be a burden, to either of us, in old age and above all, that last year of her life, she'd very often say, "Honey, I'm asking God, not to take me, until, you're strong enough, to handle it!" As I've mentioned earlier. Well, I just need to share this with you, because it's so rich and so true! And I witnessed it and I lived it and I need to share it and please, enjoy it! Don't let it upset you, in any way. It was a beautiful thing, actually, as I look back on it . . .

My Mothers own words, resonated within me, from that moment, in the car, en-route, to meet her, at the emergency room, that last night. Okay, I told myself, "You need not be, a hypocrite and buck Mums, lifelong prayer requests!" So, yes! As it turned out, we lost two Mothers, in fifteen days time, in August of 1994. Eleanor, on the 10th, Celene, on the 25th.

People, who attended the funeral of my Mum, would stop me, out and about and many requested, again and again, my tribute, "Ode to Mother," be mailed to them, for they were touched by it. I would, like to share that tribute, with you and I will share it, at the end, of this entire writing. So, I did give my Mum, her tribute, at the Catholic mass and it was beautiful and I thank the God, for His words!

Well, in the fullness of time, I needed to, clean all of her belongings and clean, out her apartment, so I did take my time, cleaning her apartment.

I paid rent, for three months and did the job, completely alone. When I needed to sell items, I had Alex or close friends, only, helping me. Dad had come in, in September of 1994, from Florida, to take Billy and Billy's belongings, for relocation to Palm Bay, Florida.

Mum and Billy, were never close, ever, because of their own issues and his allegiance, to our Father and his new life, with Maria. My brother himself, had made the choice, of a new life, when his three children, were six, three and in-vitro! Billy had been an atheist, for a very long time. So, change, without a God, to answer to, or to live for . . . the glory of, was not important to him.

The way we felt, was that, he had divorced Debby, this is how Mother and I felt . . . and had left the children and that they now, had a stepfather, that was Billy's choice, but thank goodness, my sister-in-law, my brothers first wife, Debby . . . FIRST wife, named Debby, was open minded, to the idea of Mum and myself and Alex, still cultivating relationships, with her and my two nephews and niece. She was a good person and I will always love my first sister-in-law Debby. She did give us, access to the children. I will forever, love Debby and respect her, for being a caring, sister-in-law and even though, we've lost touch, I still love and care, for her . . . and the now grown children, my friends, from the bottom of my heart!

The years between, Mums death and the summer of 2006, twelve years, in all, were quite routine here, in my life, in my marriage and with Alex and not very noteworthy, except to say, that in 2003, Alex suffered a horrible bout, of prostate cancer, himself and had to have, radical prostatectomy and I stood by him. That was huge.

And then, I became a volunteer worker, with the Friendly Visitors, of Connecticut. During those years, from Mums death, until 2006, I also became affiliated with, Let's Help A Veteran, DeVanno, Grillo, Laudone, Post #1, of Scotland, Connecticut and also appeared, on the, "Let's Help Vet/Town Talk," weekly television show, on the then, Adelphia Public Access, Channel 14, of Norwich, Connecticut.

I volunteered, on that show, for four years and was a co-host, to my good friend, I call him my Italian Godfather, he was the founder of Let's Help A Veteran, he was also the founder, of the world famous, Jimmy Fund and his name was William Michael Colonna. Well, on that show, the Let's Help A Veteran/Town Talk, show, I would play TAPS, on the trumpet, each week, for the fallen, soldiers.

Two years into that show, I made arrangements, to become a certified producer and completed the course. The result became, my own, bi- monthly, one hour, call-in show, just as the Veterans, had a call-in format, on the Adelphia Public Access, on the two Mondays a month, entitled, "Various Matters, with Cynthia."

Like the Vets show and Larry King, it was a live, call-in, information and commentary show. I would scan, The Wall Street Journal, of the day, for cutting edge stories and was about two days, ahead, of the big boys, Bill O'Reilly and Larry King. As my good buddy, Bill Colonna, would say, at every end of, Let's Help A Vet/Town Talk, show," The spin stops right here, ladies and gentlemen . . . because we're BETTER, than Bill O'Reilly.

Ah, yes! Bill Colonna . . . the salt of the earth! A man, for all seasons! a good person. He's long gone now, he passed in 2006 and I miss him a great deal! But . . . we had fun . . . that you cannot imagine! We had two television shows going, but more than that, we helped people. That was very much, our mantra. I still, have people stopping me, even to this day, today, as I write to you, hoping, I will start my television appearances, again. The answer is: Yes, of course, I will and I did, I started my television show, "Various Matters," up again, just about a week ago, from when I'm speaking to you and this is April of 2008. This is 'Em, I'm speaking to you on, Thursday, April 24, right now! 2008!

I was . . . it was . . . during the run, of the Let's Help A Veteran/Town Talk show, in the fall of 2005, to the spring of 2006, that I would meet a beautiful young man, named Drew. He was 22 years old and going on . . . 40 mentally and a relative, of one of the co-hosts. There I was, this fat, thyroid inflated, unloved, lonely, married woman, now fighting asthma, which had come on me, at 44 and I had all the steroid issues, I was dealing with and here I was, now 46 and there I am . . . what? twenty-something, years older than him?

Yet, he was more mature and stable, than any man, I had ever met! . . . And he was pursuing, me?!? His signals at first were soft and sure, but with the passage of time, he became frustrated, because I was not picking them up! Huh! When I finally did, I was ready, for our . . . sparks to fly! Drew, started showing me attention, in the fall of 2005, at the Veterans show.

He would talk to me, mostly, before and after, the shows, he attended. When I wasn't on the set, or in the booth, he'd sit next to me, in the audience. Yes, he did talk with his, grandfather and the others, but mostly, with me! He would, offer to carry my trumpet, to and from the car. On nights the weather was good; we'd stand outside, on the sidewalk, right next to each other, backs on the wall and discuss life issues. We were very compatible, in our thinking and he was so mature . . . for his age!

He would flirt, gently, with me and I would catch him, staring at me, most of the time, inside the studio. Whenever, I would wear, my sky blue mohair hat, he would place it, on his lap and gently, pet it, as if it were a kitten! Huh! Whenever we parted, he seemed to either, want to tell me, how he felt, or to kiss me . . . He would just ask me, about my husband a lot and I told him, the truth, about the marriage and all, that it was not! He'd have a smile on his face whenever we were near and . . . HARUMPH! In his own frustration, when he'd go to his car. I could tell, he was frustrated and wanted more, but could not bring himself, to ask or do, more

Cynthia.

Chapter 26

In March, of 2006, I was in the Norwichtown Mall, with Alex, on a Sunday after church, at Bee Bee's Dairy Restaurant. I had wanted another clairvoyant reading, ever since the gypsy, at the Rocky Point Amusement Park, in Rhode Island, had told me, on a seventh grade trip, "You will be, one of the ten, most richest women, in the world. You will have, 5 children, you will live a long life."

Since none of those things, had yet happened, I always told myself, that someday, I would want to update, on that information I really never believed the gypsy, but curiosity, being what it is and on this particular Sunday, in early March, of 2006, the opportunity, to speak to a clairvoyant was posted, on a sign "Psychic Faire." It was put on, by a shop called, Delilah's and she, had rented another space and put in, purple curtain booths, to divide, the half dozen psychics at the faire.

As I walked in, I asked, "Do you have a clairvoyant?" The hostess told me, most used tarot cards, then she said, "Asher, could read you without cards!" "Please!" I said. I told Alex, to wait in the car, for me, it would be

$20.00 for a 20 minute reading. A beautiful man stepped out, from the last booth, at the right. He was my height and of slender build. He was wearing, a black three piece suit, a black tie, a yarmulke and had four white strings, flowing downward, over his pant legs. The strings were probably, properly aligned, over the fronts and backs, of his legs. "Hello, I'm Asher," he said.

We walked into his booth and he showed me a seat, next to a small table, with purple cloth, also. He took the deck, of tarot cards, in his hand and I said, "No, please, don't use cards, the lady said, you can do a clairvoyant reading, that is what I would like, please." He set the cards, down gently and said, "Give me both of your hands, palms up, please." He gazed into my hands, for about 30 seconds, then closed them and said, "Who is the younger man, who is the greener grass, for you?"

I was floored! I nearly slid, off the chair and tears came, into my eyes. Instead of 20 minutes, I was there . . . an hour and he laid out, my life, until that date, with pinpoint accuracy. He suggested, I email Drew and let him know, I was very interested. It took me a few days, to muster the courage, to do so and I finally did. Drew's responses, were short and sweet, yet even though, we connected in person and possibly, could have become involved, his mother, daughter of one of the Vets Show, co-hosts, kept a tight noose, around his neck. She would, find our emails and throw, huge fits and tell her father, to tell me, to leave her son, a 22 year old man, alone! How unfair, to me, for he also, wanted to pursue involvement.

After several months, of drama, I decided, I could not get involved with a man, of any age, who had to answer to his mother . . . again! I had been there, done that, with Alex. The last thing, I needed, was to get into, another narcissistic, controlling, atmosphere. All through these months, from March through July, 2006, I would consult Asher, on a regular basis. He tried to help me, navigate, cultivating a relationship, with Drew, until I saw, it had to stop. Soon, he told me, there would be another man, "He will be three years older and you already know him." That was all he could say.

I had an appointment, on July 16, 2006, to have my hair, cut and colored. How could I know, as I lay there, with my head, in that same familiar sink, hair being washed, styled, by Tom, for 25 years, that what, I am about to share with you, would happen.

I was thinking of another sad moment, my husband was putting me through, his condescending ways, when all at once, I felt choked, in my throat and tears, welling up, in my eyes. "What's wrong, Cindy?" Tom said, while scrubbing my hair, "Oh Tom, you don't want to know, it's my burden, just please, make my hair, beautiful!" When the color and cut, was done, I walked to the door. Tom asked me again, what, was I so sad about? As I turned the door knob, to exit the salon, just as I had done, for 25 long years, Tom beckoned me, to return to talk.

I broke down, sobbing, in huge amounts, of tears and told him, just what I had been enduring, in my marriage, to my husband. He looked so stunned! "I thought you and Alex, were close, the perfect couple!" Tom said. Well, when I told him, the truth, about all I had endured, all he said was, "Oh, God! Cindy, listen, let's go out to dinner, soon, oh, my God! We both, want the same thing, I can't believe, God has brought us together, this way!" I left with a dinner date in mind.

And so, the date of our dinner, July 18th, came. I told my husband, that afternoon "I'm going out, to meet a man tonight and I want you, to be the first to know, not the last, because I've seen, what that is like, when my father left for Marie, and I'll not be a hypocrite!" Well, at that, my husbands eyes, welled up, with just a few tears, as he peered, through our dining room, sliding glass door, windows, into the woods, behind our house. I said, "You know what? Those tears, are for yourself, your pride, not for me!" he said nothing.

That night, I met Tom, at the Harp and Dragon Pub, in Norwich, he was so, handsome and beautiful, in my eyes. He had convinced me, on the day, of the hair appointment, that we both wanted, the same things, in life, now. He was a 14 year, divorcee and single, having just ended, an 8 year relationship, with a woman, in New Jersey. They fought too much, he told me and it, was long distance he said, so it had to be over.

Well, ladies and gentlemen, let me tell you, this was like, an intense affair, with a man, I knew, for 25 years, who was exactly, three years older, as Asher, had predicted. It was, my first affair and me, I don't ever, . . . thought, never thought, in my world, in my Catholic world, my staunch world, something I never thought, I would ever, have done. I didn't know that I, would be swept up, it . . . and this thing, with Tom, nearly consumed me. It was crazy! It was insane! I could, go on and on, but I don't want, to trash him, 'em, because we, did have a good friendship, for 25 years, prior to this insane, 'em, short-lived, 'em, sexual affair. Need I just say that, when it was over, I was totally lost, adrift, at sea, with no safe harbors, in sight . . .

I decided to buy a convertible car. In my mind, I told myself, I was remembering back, to the '77, Triumph Spitfire, that Dad had bought me, so I thought, you know, in time, I would like to buy, 'em, perhaps, a convertible car, to try and reconnect, with my husband, Alex. Since he'd never, driven in one, I thought, it would be, nice! So, I just thought we, should just move, in that direction and I needed, to reconnect with, God, so I made a, good confession and I, for now, need to just ask you, to please, bear with me, because . . . there are, other events, which I will, present and when, we are done, with this first dissertation, on my life, on my statement, on the title of the book, the very title of the book, when I am done, with this entire, first dissertation, I promise you, all will become clear, crystal clear.

Cynthia.

Chapter 27

The pain and rejection, I felt from Tom, was hard to bear. Not only, had he swooped down me, at the lowest, weakest point in my marriage, intellectually, he had only used me, for sex and jealousy, as he had no intention, of ending, his eight year, on and off again, out-of-state romance, with Lisa. I was deeply, hurt and disillusioned, by him. He, for the sake of sexual jollies, had violated, a 25 year, stylist, client, relationship, not to mention a friendship! In which, we could always, laugh and joke around, as just buddies . . . all those years! I had sat . . . in his salon chair . . . he had full knowledge; I was very staunch, in my Roman Catholicism.

Heck, I'd say rosaries for, years . . . while my perms, or hair colors were being processed. When he always tried, to give me magazines, to read, for a quarter of a century, he'd say, to me, "Do you want to read this, or that?" and I'd say, "No, thanks Tom, I'm going to pray, the rosary, while I'm waiting, instead." Huh! When I didn't know, how to continue in my marriage, for lack of intimacy, kindness, or . . . and peace, before Tom and now, after Tom, I thought, "Okay . . . what shall I do?!?" once I've made, a good confession, to try and bring, Alex and me, closer together?

It was a Monday morning, about one week after, the tryst with Tom, first started, July the 24th of 2006, to be exact. Diane called me, from Westerly Hospital, Emergency Room. She had been flown in, overnight, from Block Island, Rhode Island, due to a bad fall, off approximately, forty foot embankment, on a late night walk, in the salt air.

She had every test, in the book and thank God, she was only, badly bruised, very lucky, indeed! She asked me, to come, to that ER and stay, with her, until her husband, Charles, could arrive back, at about noon, with the Jeep, on the Point Judith Ferry? Of course, I could! I took a quick, "navy shower," brushed my teeth, dressed and dashed, out the door. It was about 8:30 a.m. In about, 45 minutes, I was with her, at Westerly Hospital.

It was a beautiful, warm, summers morning, so they let her sit outside, in a wheelchair, until her husband, would arrive. I was so happy, to see, she was not hurt badly. I went to the McDonald, in Westerly, Rhode Island and got us, breakfast and coffee. We sat and chatted, until Charles arrived, about 11:30 a.m. We talked about, all our girl stuff, but mostly, how Tom, had been a total cad, to use me, only for sex and to, make the woman, Lisa, in New Jersey, jealous enough, to restart their, dysfunctional, long distance, romance. She said, "Cin, what are you going to do, now, about you and Alex?!?"

"I'm going to buy, a convertible car, on the way home!" I said. "You are?" she retorted. "Yes, I'm going to get a Mazda Miata, he's never ridden, in a 'rag top,' it will be fun, he'll enjoy it and maybe, we can become, closer and get along, on car trips, in it!" I said, with hope in my heart. Charles arrived and as I waved, goodbye to them, I thought of going, directly, to New London Motors, Lincoln, Mercury, Mazda, to find the car.

I got onto, I-95 South and headed, to the dealership. I remember thinking, as I crossed, the Gold Star Bridge, between Groton and New London, Connecticut, that the next time, I would cross it, would be, twice, on a test drive . . . huh! With my top down, in the Miata, I would buy. Looking hurried and not, at all, well put together, due to, dashing out, for Diane . . . it really didn't matter, that I had, no makeup on, no pretty dress, or no well coiffed, hairdo. I was so sour, on men! My Dad, for rejecting me, all those, past many years, my husband, rejecting and demeaning me, with the help, of his brood of vipers, family, all those years . . . and now Tom! A friend! And my stylist, of 25 years . . . whose rejection and betrayal and use of me, as a sex object, and a jealousy factor, for Lisa?!? Made me feel, very bitter, indeed!

I pulled up, to the front door, of the New London Motors and parked. Right outside, the front door, were two men, both smoking cigarettes. One, very ordinary looking, the other . . . adorable! What

Luck! When the adorable one, approached me, "Hello," he said. I told him, "I want to buy, that black, Mazda Miata, over there!" as I pointed, to it. "Great! I'll get the keys and we'll, go for a test drive!" he said.

When he returned, he had a business card, with someone else's name, crossed out and his name, hand written, above it. I put out my hand, I said, "I'm Cynthia." He shook my hand and said, "I'm Anthony." Oh! Well! I put the card, in my purse and he, drove me through New London, across the Gold Star Bridge, to the Groton side. While crossing, he challenged me! To find, the gas cap release! Saying, "You'll never find it, I couldn't, someone, had to show me!" I said, "You don't know me, I will find it, pull over and I'll . . . prove it!"

With that, he flashed me, the most precious, effervescent, smile and twinkle, in his eye. Instantly . . . my mind began to wander, over and over, "Who are you? And where, have you been . . . all my life?!?" When I first saw him, on the sidewalk, I became enamored, with his looks and his mannerisms and now, in the car, his personality, had totally smitten me. I now know, what love, at first sight, is because, that is how he impacted me.

It took me, all of about 30 seconds, to find, the gas cap release! "How did you, do that?" he wondered with his impish smile and beautiful, Adonis face. "Easy!" I told him, "You don't know me, I am very, smart and ingenious!" With that, I hopped, into the driver's seat, driving on the road, of Groton, along the Thames River, near Dad and Rickover's Sub, Nautilus.

We had great conversation, I told him about, the sub and its place, in my life. He was, himself, so interesting, not to mention, gorgeous, that time just flew by, in his company. Before we crossed, the Gold Star Bridge, again, I said, "I want you, to drive me back, Anthony and show me, what my car can do!"

He was, an excellent driver and took, command, of the auto and the road. I loved, every moment of it! Back in the office, I sat, on the edge of my seat, directly across from him, at his desk. I looked, all around, to find clues, of his personality. The items, he had, on his desk and shelf. He had a Doberman picture, in a pewter, heart frame a drum set, in a rectangle frame, a mini book, about fast cars, Nivea hand lotion, on the shelf and posters and brochures, of the autos, he was selling.

On his desk, were three manila folders, neatly stacked, yet fanned out, for each client, he had a contract for. Well, I sat and admired his every move! When all the paperwork, was done and he, looked up, into my staring eyes, I almost blurted out, "Who are you? And where, have you been, all my life?!?" Instead, we both asked, if the other was married. He said, he was not now, or ever married and when, I wondered why . . . he said, "Well, at 38, I'm still . . . haven't met, the right woman . . . yet!"

He handed me, another of his cards and put, his cell phone number, on it, in case, I needed to reach him. I told him, I would be back, with the bank check, in two days. The conversation got more personal, I told him why, I wanted the car, honestly. He seemed sad, for me. I found out he was raised right, in his life, with his parents, as a Roman Catholic, like me. I could see, he was raised well, for he was kind, intellectual, articulate, respectful and had manners and an, impeccable way, he presented himself.

As I stood, to leave, I wanted to tell him, on the spot, how I felt, about him! He had swept me, off my feet! Without even trying! Thinking of him, made me happy inside, for the first time in two decades! . . . Or so, about someone! How I longed, for the two days, until I could see him again . . . to go by!

Cynthia.

Chapter 28

When Alex came home, from fishing that day, I told him, about Diane and about the Miata, I wanted to buy. He, being the question box, of all, I ever wanted, instead of just giving it, to me, said, "Let's look around, at other convertibles." "No!" I said, flatly. "Do you want, to try and get closer, together . . . I want that car, not any other and I want it, so we can go for, 'drive dates,' and to try and put Tom, and our, marriage problems, behind us, it will be fun, just wait and see, we'll love it, day and night. Night rides, with the top down, are the best!" I explained.

He didn't take it any further. I got the car loan, on my own, for $25,000.00 and the 26th of July 2006, we both went to, in my '71 Porsche, 911 T Coupe, to pick up my new, Mazda Miata. As we pulled in, it was at the front door, gleaming and ready, to go! We parked the Porsche and a couple, of the other salesmen, inquired about it.

We showed them, the entire car, inside and also, the engine, which was changed, to a new, '74 Carerra block, with 6 Weber carburetors. They were amazed, at the car, which I call, "Pearl the Porsche," because of her, pearl essence, color and it looks like, it is only about, three years old and she's got, about, only 46,500 miles, on that day . . . original miles!

Well soon, Anthony came out to greet us and I, was telling the others, about Pearl's story . . . It began, on a day, my cousins husband, was taking, his ladder and painting equipment, to his truck, one last Spring day, in 2004. As he was putting his things, in the truck, the elderly lady, the homeowner, shot out, of her back door and screamed, at what he thought, was the lawn guy!

She was about, 80 years old and very vibrant. She screamed, over the lawnmower sound, in Polish! To the lawnmower man, which made my cousin, approach him, afterwards, saying, "What is that lady, screaming to you, in Polish, about?" The man answered, "UGH! That's my mother, everytime; I come here, for the last 15 years, she screams, for me to . . . 'Take that, GD car, out of my garage!"

What kind of car is it? Steven said, to which the man answered, "Come in, I'll show it to you!" It was, a completely closed garage, no windows, at all. There was a mound, of old blankets, quilts and afghans, on top. When the man, Henry, removed them, the florescent lights, lit up the Porsche. Steven got weak, in the knees "That's beautiful! Is it for sale?" he asked.

"The price is $15,000.00 cash!" Henry said, "Only two other people, are interested and they, only want to pay, $12,000.00 cash! It's $15,000.00 cash, or it can sit!" That evening, Steven told me, about the car. I had always wanted another sports car, since the Triumph, had been totaled. Alex was in agreement, to buy it.

Three months and a matter, of a few thousand dollars, later, she is a "Pearl the Porsche" The offers started, coming in as soon, as I drove her. The current bid, as of this writing is $150,000.00 because she is one of a kind, truly, a priceless Pearl! So, okay! Yes! Again! I'm spoiled! I admit it! Yet, I have never had the one, thing that eludes me, true love and happiness, I shouldn't be bleak, but it is something, I still desire! As Garfunkel once said, "Looking for the right one, will the right one . . . come along?!?"

Sorry, of course, readjustment, so yes . . . I picked up, that new Miata, that day, in 2006 and had the pleasure, of enjoying it, with Alex, many days and nights, that summer.

On August 23rd, 2006 as I shall say, I was down, in the dumps, because Alex, had stood me up, coming home, to go out, in the Miata . . . for fishing! Which upset me! I decided to go, to the Harp and Dragon Pub, in downtown, Norwich. I sat there, sipping my merlot, wine and feeding, my loneliness, when the phone suddenly rang. "Hello, Cynthia? This is Anthony," we talked a few minutes, I hadn't heard, or seen him since I picked up, that Miata. He asked if I wanted, to buy Yankee tickets, for the next night, in New York City. I told him, I didn't know, where Alex was, yet, or if he, would want to buy them.

I offered to buy one . . . and drive Anthony, to the game, the next night. Anthony told me, he needed to call a few other people first, we said goodbye. Well, who, sashays into, the Harp and Dragon, but Tom! On one of his, off again, days and or nights, from Lisa, in New Jersey Now, myself, feeling lonely, rejected, yet again, by Alex and needing, human touch and intimacy, I took him, yet again, the last time, in fact, back to his apartment, where, we, how do you say, "got physical!" again . . .

I stayed all night, which made Alex, furious, yet, he only had himself, to blame, for again, putting himself, his hobby, before us, for the, let's see . . . MILLIONTH TIME! Anyhow, I decided, never to bed Tom, or any other man, again . . . unless or until, in a committed relationship. That would, become my new focus, with regards to, the sexual, physical, side of life.

I'm not into self-sex, never really was, I am traditional, I want a man, in my bed and trust me, he receives, a woman. Soon, Norwich Free Academy, started the '06-'07, school year. Alex and I were back, in our quiet, doldrums, brother and sister, who don't get along, marriage, sleeping, still, in separate beds, for fifteen plus, long, lonely, love starved, years . . . for me!

I was, behaving myself and being, the doting, wife, as best I could. One warm day, 8 October, 2006, to be exact, we went out after school, so I could get ice cream. The check engine, light, came on, in the Mazda Miata, as he was driving. He said, "I'm going to drive, to, New London Motors! This is bullshit! It's the, second time and there are; only 600 miles, on this piece of shit . . . you paid, $25,000.00 for!" Well, that did it!

Once again, the thing I liked, I wanted, was shit! I was so disgusted, with him; I played possum and faked sleep, until we got there. After visiting the service department, he came around, and announced, "I'll be, It'll be a half an hour, wait," To which, I said, "Okay, I'll nap here, in the car. "Okay I'm going to see, Anthony." his reply. "Tell him, I said hello!" in my sleepiness.

I must have dosed off . . . suddenly, because, the next thing, I was aware of, was, a voice . . . "Hello, Sunshine!" I opened my eyes, to see Anthony, at my door. "Hello, Anthony . . . " I said, with my heart leaping, for joy, at the very, sight, of him! I got out, stood up and he gave me, a friendly hug, hello. Wow! Awesome! I'll never forget it! Question was . . . would I ever, receive . . . another?

Cynthia.

Chapter 29

The three of us, walked over, to the sidewalk. I said, "How are you . . . Anthony? To which, he explained, that the "Big Dig," behind the dealership, a true blast zone, construction site, on that day, would be his new endeavor. "What, he would be leaving New London Motors?" I thought . . . As soon, as the new building, was up and leasing space? Then I said, "What will you be doing, in business there, Anthony?"

He said, "I'm opening, a recording studio, modeling and talent agency and a magazine, called "TWIST," to start and then, eventually, I want to pursue, television and radio, but . . . I haven't, found the right partner yet. With that, I said, nothing and went to my wallet, to produce, my television producer, certification which, I always carry. When I got back on the sidewalk, I handed it, to him, to which I added, "Not only, have I mastered television, I was in the print media, for six years, I've tried many businesses, alone, through the years, I've never had a partner. Would you, consider me?" "Yes," he said, "Alex, what do you think?" I inquired. "Let's talk about it," he said.

So there, on the sidewalk, the three of us, discussed, my partnering, with Anthony. Within a few days time, I was doing research, obtaining domain names, producing some, graphic support and having daily, luncheon meetings, with Anthony, on his lunch hour, from New London Motors. We were, intellectually similar and this was, the basis, of our getting along, so well, at the early stages, of beginning to build, his dream and my desire, of a successful business, he named, Star Power Productions.

I soon learned he was a professional drummer, who knew the studio system, well and had played, for several, famous recording artists. His business savvy and all, his other attributes, made him, the quintessential figure, of something, I was beginning to envision, as a major force, to be coming, into the industry. How sweet, it would be! I would be able to work, side by side, with the only man; I have ever loved, at first sight! . . . And spend huge amounts, of time, with him! Honestly, that was, all I hoped for, all I thought possible, because, there I was, eight years older and in a stagnant yet cloistered, marriage, out of shape, overweight and had never, been the, "pretty girl," I can, look striking and attractive, I knew that, but, any thought of ever hoping, Anthony, would desire me, as a woman, was a sheer fantasy, at first.

After about, four weeks, of trying to work around, his New London Motors, schedule, we decided, to start looking for another location, because the new building, would take, several more months, to complete. The two of us, with a friend, of his, named Mark, looked at, several spaces. We decided, on a former Laundry Mat, in Groton, near, Electric Boat Shipyard, division of, General Dynamics.

We signed the lease, with the owner, Dennis, at the rate of, $1,200.00 a month, with first and security, as deposit the place, was loaded, with old, decrepit, washers and dryers. Dennis told us, he would give us, 90 days, rent free, to build, to suit, our needs, at our expense! He promised, to empty it out, within a week . . . Well, that week, turned into several, approximately 6 weeks, so now, half of our, "free period," of 12 weeks, was gone!

He was, very concrete sequential, in his attitude. When we tried to remind him, we needed to, get in and start our construction, of the studio, he was busy, always, because he owned many properties, in Connecticut and Rhode Island. The six week wait, became, extremely, nerve wrecking! Anthony, had left the New London Motors, for the first week of November, to devote, all of his time, to the studio . . . and now, we were completely stalled, by the landlord!

Anthony, not having a company car, was renting, a yellow, Jeep C-J, from a friend, week to week. That became very expensive, along with the fact, that, he had a cottage, in Old Lyme, Connecticut, he was renting and needed, his own living expenses. So there we were, trying to open the studio, with the landlord, preventing us from getting into it, to put up all the walls, ceilings and then, paint, carpet, and all the necessary fixtures, to turn a huge run down chasm, into a state of the art, elegant recording studio.

Anthony, decided, we needed to buy and sell, used cars, as a sideline, until, the studio could open. I put in $16,000.00 of my money and he put in, whatever he had. We bought 9 used cars, to help defray, his expenses and to try to stockpile, some funds, to pay rent and utilities, once we would open. I would drive, every day, from my home, in Lisbon, Connecticut, to his cottage, in Old Lyme, Connecticut, where we, would brainstorm and plan, Star Powers, future.

That was only part, of what we would do, because we were in a stagnant, holding, pattern, to get into the building, to renovate. We would go out, to eat and try, to network and scout talent, at malls, or wherever we went.

Since, I was so in love, with him, from the moment, I saw him, I loved the long afternoons and evenings, we'd spend together. I hated, to leave him and go, home. Our friendship, partnership, was totally platonic, on his part, but I was falling, faster and deeper, in love with Anthony, every passing moment, hour, and day.

I tried, to leave him once, because the pain, of wanting him, to want me, as a woman, was like a malignancy, which was drawing, devouring my soul, from the inside. My love, for him was surely and sadly, unrequited. One day, I showed up and told him I was going to end, being his partner, but . . . I never told him, why! I was suffering, because loving him, was killing me! Not softly . . . but deadly!.. Inside!

I returned, that night, with Diane and Charles, to have Anthony sign, a promissory note, for $16,000.00 with them, as witnesses. He signed it, hesitantly. The next day, I went back, to apologize, for leaving him and to try, to explain to him, that he would be, just fine, without me, that I only, wanted to be his friend, not business partners.

Tears came into his eyes, as he told me, "I don't want another partner, I only want you, I don't care, about the money, or the business . . . I only want it with you, Cynthia!"

    I put my arm, around him, as he sat, face in hands, at the table and I told him, why I had to leave him, because it was killing me, being in love, with him and wanting him, to love me back! As a woman! Not just, a partner or friend. I told him, how hard it was, for me to know, he was seeing other women, when I would go, home at night!

    He could see, how possessive and jealous, I was and yet, to this day . . . I still don't know, why, he didn't just let me go, then. We talked, a while and he convinced me, that I could be happy, in the studio, with him. Even though, he told me, "Cynthia, you're not my type!" bluntly and very, matter-of-factly. Of course, I wasn't his type, though, I knew it! Here he was, 8 years younger and the most, beautiful man, I'd ever seen, the world over and he, had a thing for, "girls," approximately 20!

    Even though, he knew I loved him, to the pit, of my soul and as deep as my bone marrow, he didn't want, to release me, I took, that day and his tears, as hope?!? Maybe, he has a space for me, in his heart? The question was, would it be, a false hope?

Cynthia.

Chapter 30

When the drama settled, and we got back, to a place of focusing, on Star Power, all was well, with us. We'd go out, to shop and decide, what we needed, to buy for the construction phase and then, all the furnishings and equipment. Finally, the week before Christmas, Denny, Dennis, had emptied, the space.

We went to Waterford, Home Depot and I, opened a line of credit, necessary for all, we would need to build. Soon, Anthony, met some young carpenters, who would do the work and so, construction . . . began. Within a couple of weeks, there was a huge rainstorm, which showed us, the next morning, that there were huge puddles, inside the studio building and the sheetrock, on the outside wall, was saturated . . . nearly, the whole depth, of the space.

We were very upset, to discover, the puddles, inside and to see, the sheetrock, which when saturated, showed the extent, of the mold, inside the walls. Ah! Anthony was livid! He got on the phone to Dennis, insisted he fix the problems. Dennis was very cavalier and not in a hurry, to correct, the multiple leaks, of the roof, into the studio and into, the exterior wall!

Now, it was getting, to be mid to late January and construction, had to stop. Okay! Huh! So, there we were, back in his cottage, afternoons and evenings, both of us, very down trodden, over the situation. Yes, we did smoke pot . . . and party together, since we had first met, I'm not going to lie . . . I never do!

We needed, to relax and soothe, our many, frustrations and disappointments With all this, happening, on a cold January, night, I decided to bring, a box of wine, merlot, five liter, bag in the box and a bottle, of Grey Goose, Vodka, to Anthony's cabin, cottage.

Anthony was not an alcohol drinker, he would allow it, in his home, but he only, smoked marijuana, or so I thought . . . more on that later.

Anyhow, this particular night, I had been out, grocery and supply shopping and picking up his laundry, at the Snow White Laundromat, in Old Lyme, earlier in the day. I was so disgusted, with Dennis and my heart, was heavy, each day, as I tried to be, with Anthony, loving him more and more, only to see, that more and more and more . . . I was just, a business and financial entity, in his life. He had no emotion, for me and I started, to feel sorry, for myself!

I made a screwdriver and drank it, in 30 seconds! I then, started slamming down, the merlot wine! I could see Anthony, was becoming aggravated that I was getting, extremely drunk and then, he told me so. That was it! I saw red! I was, totally intoxicated and demanded, that he end, our business relationship, yet again! I begged him, to make love to me, in my drunken stupor!

He said, "No, Cynthia, you're drunk, you need, to sober up and go home! I'm going for a ride, you are out of control!" As he, tried to leave, I blocked him, repeatedly, which made him furious! He would duck, and twirl and try, to get past me, to the door. I ripped, his hooded sweatshirt, right off, of him and insisted, and insisted, we have sex, "Right Now! You need, to have sex with me, Anthony! Just, this once . . . and you'll, never see me again! Please . . . just make love to me and I'll go away . . . and never, bother you again . . . ever!"

Soon, Anthony did get out, the door and was gone, about 20 minutes. In that 20 minutes, I did all, I could, to remove or destroy, everything; I had bought, that day . . . or any day, for that matter. I emptied food, in the garbage, beverages in the sink, shampoos and the like, down the drain and even, dumped ten pounds, of ice melt crystals, on the front stoop!

When he returned, the Tasmanian devil, in me, began to destroy, other things, I had given him, such as belts, clothing, whatever I saw, which made me feel, I meant nothing, more, than a money source, to him. When he, came back and he screamed, "Cynthia! What is wrong with you! What are you . . . what have you done! I only went out, for a pack of cigarettes! You need to sober up and go home!" Well, that only made me, madder!

I ripped, a poster he had, about achieving goals, A to Z, off the wall and began, to insist, yet again, he . . . quote . . . "Have sex with me!" unquote. Again, he tried to leave, I blocked and shoved him! When he got out, he went, to a neighbor's cottage. The neighbor, called the Old Lyme Police. Soon, three officers and a German shepherd were on the scene. Anthony came back in, he tried to have the police, leave me alone, with him, to sober up, because, I was totally drunk!

The police, did not want him, to have to deal with me, anymore and of course, I did not, want to leave, because, the drunken, spoiled, her majesty, the baby, still wanted, Anthony's sex! What a horrible mess, I had made, but I didn't care . . . an officer, with the name tag, Gunn, stood by the kitchen. I belligerently, went up to him and took my right, index finger and jabbed him, several times, on the badge!

"So you're Mr. Gunn, are you? . . . you don't know, who you're fucking with, I am a Gunn, I am, Cynthia Gunn and I've lived, in the motherland, so don't give me, any of your, macho, Celtic, bullshit! It won't work, with me!" With that, officer Gunn, spun me around, slammed my chest, up against the bathroom door, turned my head to the left, pressed my skull, into the door, pulled first, my right then, my left arm backward and said, "You're under arrest."

Another officer, assisted, in handcuffing me, they put me, in those cuffs, so tight, I felt as though, my wrists bones, were splitting! They pulled me, out of the cottage, backwards, by the cuffed wrists, which was excruciating! The dog was going nuts!

When they opened, the back cruiser door, they spun me around, like a top and pushed my head down, to my waist height and shoved me, in the car . . . sideways! Anthony and the neighbors were watching, in disbelief. He tried to tell the officers, not to arrest me, that all I needed, was to sober up! His pleas were ignored. I had created, my own Monster, unleashed her and then, she tried to take, a police officer, over the psychological coals! All shit faced and fallen down, drunk! I had no one to blame, but myself, or . . . did I!?!

Cynthia.

Chapter 31

The Old Lyme Police took me, to the Westbrook, State Police barracks. I had all my belongings, handbag, jewelry and the like, taken away, from me. I was photographed, fingerprinted and allowed, my one call . . . I was too drunk, to make it! They, called Alex and told him, to come and collect me! They took me, to the basement and put me, in a small cage . . . not even a cell, with a wooden platform, only, to sit on, I couldn't even lie down!

In about, an hour and a half, Alex came and took me home. I didn't want, to talk about it, I only told him, that Anthony and I, occasionally fought and that, I had too much, to drink and became too combative. I could not, at that time, tell Alex, the truth, that I was head over heels, in love, with Anthony and how, it was consuming me, body, mind, heart, soul and conscience.

Since my car, was still at Anthony's cottage, the next morning, my friend, Diane, brought me, to retrieve it. Anthony was awake and so, I bid her, a due, on the promise, that I was only going to, pick up the car and go, straight home. That was not, at all, my intention. What I hoped for, instead, was that Anthony would, forgive me, for becoming, drunk and disorderly and I, would promise, never, to become so, again . . .

We made our peace, that day and decided, to continue, as business partners. So now, it was, mid to late January, of 2007 and we had, the leaky roof, moldy building, to overcome, with Dennis, that became, the focus and we both, were on, our best behaviors and kept, our eye, on the prize, the eventual opening, of our studio.

Dennis, did do, a quick fix, on the roof and by the end, of January . . . the 31st . . . to be exact . . . all was looking well. It was getting to be, about 8:30

p.m. On that night, we had smoked, marijuana and had our, "good buddy," fun, getting along, so well, after the huge, "blow out," when I was drunk, a couple of weeks, before.

Anthony stood up and came, to my side, of the table. He took off, his baseball cap and gave me, the most tender, short, sweet, kiss, directly on the lips, with his beautiful, drummers hands, on either side, of my face, "Cynthia, this is because, you have been, a good girl, now, we can become . . . partners, with benefits . . . " Again, he gently kissed my lips, but parted them, with his beautiful, sensual, desirable, tongue. I moved in closer, for a deeper kiss and he, softly, gently, parted lips, yet stayed, face to face. "You deserve a chip! I will give you, partners, with benefits, once a month, you have, my word and you may choose, when, to call in, your chip . . . "

Stunned . . . yet, totally consumed, by his, total being and physical prowess, I was speechless . . . he took me, by the hand and led me, to his bed. He placed, all the pillows, in proper positions, gave my upper body, proper support and then, removed, my top and bra, kissing me softly, yet . . . quite parted . . . in our lips, . . . he removed my underpants, slowly-oh-so-slowly, down my side, over knees, past shins, over feet and placed them, off to the side.

My short, brown wool skirt was still on me. He climbed up, to me; face to face, said nothing . . . I closed my eyes and waited, for him to, "take me." In an instant, I remembered, something, he had said, the night of the arrest . . . and my drunkenness, "If I decide to, take you, I take you, you don't . . . take me . . . "

His words, from my horrific night, now, comforted me, as he kissed me, lightly, on my lips, forehead, right, then left, nipple, then . . . he . . . kissed me, gently, on the belly button, once and once, above the pubic bone, area . . . and then, as I shuddered, not wanting to say a word . . . only . . . to experience him, as a man, finally . . . he took, his right thumb and gently, rubbed, my female, external, sex organ . . . to the left and the right, softly, gently, briefly, until I had, an internal, combustion orgasm, the likes of which, cannot be, described . . .

Soon, in a minute, of no contact, he was back! Ah! It was, a silent return, slipping my brown wool skirt, upward, yet again! To lay . . . gently and directly, on top of my body. I FELT him, his manhood, on top of my body and belly. I didn't know, how I would be, able to handle him, for he was so, beautiful, so large and in total charge, of our encounter.

Soon, he was, spreading my legs, for his entrance, into my body. I needed him, inside me . . . I wanted him, inside me and when, he entered me, I thought I would go insane! in ecstasy! He, took total control, of both of our bodies, occasionally, he would dip down and briefly, kiss me with closed lips . . . and then, thrust inside, more tenderly and still, deeper.

He knew, I was lonely and neglected, as a woman, for so long . . . he was kind and considerate, to make sure, I was most comfortable, yet . . . deeply accessible, readjusting, the pillows, beneath my body, while giving me, the full and complete, measure of his manhood . . . and CONSIDERABLE blending, of our two bodies, as ME, living, breathing, with HIM as one . . . loving, feeling . . . UNTIL . . . on a plane of physical and earthly . . . BLISS, we met!

There was no hurry, no rush, he truly decided, to, "treat me," to a chip, as he called it, "Partners with, benefits!" When I could tell, he soon, would be done . . . after a long while of the, intense, physical sharing, he gave me, I dug, my fingernails, into his sculpted, Adonis derriere', not wanting him, to EVER remove himself, from inside of me. "Cynthia, STOP! You're hurting me!" he said, softly.

I removed my fingernails and waited, we both found, the beat, the rhythm, the groove, the zone, that brought us . . . to . . . the moment, of ECSTACY! Oh! My God! How, would I ever, live another day . . . without him . . . NOW!

I was, elated, and scared, at the same time. He kissed me, on the lips, gently and left the bedroom. I reached down, to feel his seed, draining, from my body . . . It was, not there! I got, upset and then mad and then indignant. I leapt, from the bed, to find him, in the bathroom, still in his beautiful, full strength, of manhood.

"Where's the DNA, Anthony!?! What did you do, with it!?! He took off, a condom . . . I never even knew, was involved and, threw it, in the garbage. You'll have another chip, next month, Cynthia, partners . . . with benefits!

I was afraid, to say, or do, anything Instead, I thanked him, for being, so physically kind and generous, to me. I really thought, I'd have to wait . . . until late February, for my next chip. I got dressed and left, soon after. He was very much, a gentleman and very sweet, after our encounter. "I'll see you tomorrow, Cynthia, be careful, you will see a deer, on the road tonight, on the way home! So, be careful, driving!" Anthony said.

With that, I did, drive home and did see, a deer, cross my path. Yes, I was, an, "in-tune person," some, may call . . . psychic . . . but now, so was Anthony! I was, TOTALLY HAPPY, for the first night, of my life!

Cynthia.

Chapter 32

The next day, 1 February, 2007, I couldn't wait . . . to reach Anthony, at his cottage! How, would I ever, be able, to contain myself? . . . Now, after, what I considered, lovemaking!?! Even though . . . HE did NOT! I was happy, sad, scared and hopeful, all at the same time!

Happy, he could stand me, finally, bodily . . . sad, he was not, really, attracted to me . . . remember, "Not his type!" scared he would never, give up, another, "Chip, to me, ever . . . again?!?" and instead, I'd have to watch, his parade, of twenty-something, women . . . come, into view . . . yet, again! But, I had a small, mustard seed, of hope, only, that maybe . . . he felt-something, inside for me.

In the dark, away from . . . the world and its demands, I was hopeful, I had channeled my love . . . into his body! When HE, made LOVE with ME! That night, 1 February 2007, I did ask, for my chip! I said, "Anthony, today, is a new month, February, may I please, have my chip . . . TODAY!"

He agreed, but remained and reminded me, that . . . I would have to wait, until March, for another! I didn't care, I wanted him, I needed him . . . How I loved him! And, so, yes, he did give me my chip, in the same manner, yet, something . . . was different! The night before, was a surprise, I had NO IDEA . . . he was going to, "take me," to the bed.

This chip night, I knew, he would, keep his word, but it would be, because I had asked, for him, not because, he had decided, for me. Yes, it was all and more, yes it was, intense and more, yes, he gave me his DNA. How I hoped, that God, in his heaven, would bless me, with a BABY . . . of Anthony's. That night, I saw a change, in him. I wasn't sure, what it was, I only hoped, it was, in a positive direction, toward me, toward a feeling of us, as man and woman, above and beyond, business partners.

I was again, scared to ask, any questions. I went, directly home, silently, yet, more content and fulfilled, than I ever had thought, possible, in my own, lifetime.

The next day, he announced, we would be, meeting his mother, for lunch, the following week, in Providence. I was so thrilled, yet, cautious, I was scared, to think, he wanted her, to meet me, as a woman, in his life. I told myself, "Two glorious encounters, chips, now, I'll meet his mother . . . What then?!? I dared, not, think ahead.

That evening Anthony told me, he would have to, return, the Jeep, to his friend, I said, "Then, we'll buy you a Mercedes Benz, tomorrow!" We made plans, to visit, the Carriage House, of New London, Connecticut, the next day. He drove, a 2000, silver, SLK, for a day and we bought it!

We had decided, to build, a fleet for Star Power Productions, in the downtime until Dennis, would completely fix, the roof, in Groton. Anthony and I, decided we needed, a 2000, white, four door, E320 Benz, which I, would drive and a black, 2004, SLK, JoAnn, his Mum, could drive and a silver, 2007 SUV, that Anthony's stepfather, David . . . also known as, "Sarge," could drive, all to use, as "props," for Star Power, in all arenas.

Music videos, print, commercials, etcetera. What better way, to have some nice vehicles, we could, all enjoy and use, for business, too! We made all four, car deals, within, a week and decided, to celebrate, everything, we had accomplished, so far. Prior to this decision, we had met JoAnn, at a wonderful luncheon, in a beautiful, brick building, in a fine restaurant, in downtown, Providence, Rhode Island, several days, before, we decided, to build, the Mercedes Benz, fleet!

I had, bought her, a Lenox crystal, sugar and creamer set . . . and had, taken it, to her. I had bought it, at Macy's, as a gift . . . 'Em, since my parents, Mother and Father, had taught me, that this, would be, a proper, social grace, when you're meeting someone, that you value, as a Mother, of a friend, you give them, a gracious gift!

So, there, the three of us, sat and dined, elegantly and got along, famously! Anthony and his mother, had a beautiful closeness, I didn't see, too many times . . . before in life.

JoAnn and I, she and I, excused ourselves, to the ladies room, when we first met, the very first day. There we, joked, and laughed, about the awkwardness, of public, restrooms. When we, got back to the table, I could see, Anthony, was happy, that she and I, had connected, as friends. Our friendship was one, which . . . could be, cultivated and so, we decided, to pursue it.

Hence . . . everything we decided and In celebration, of all, that Anthony and I, had decided, to do, after I met, JoAnn and the building, of the fleet, for Star Power . . . JoAnn and her husband, David, "Sarge," got tickets, to see, Howie Mandel, at the Foxwoods Casino, Fox Theatre, for Valentine weekend, of 2007.

She and I, decided, to get, two rooms, at the Mystic, Hilton. We checked in, during the afternoon, of the Mandel show. Anthony, was busy, cultivating clients, for the studio, talent and said, he would, join us, later, at the Foxwoods Casino, for food and gambling. I really didn't know, if, I'd . . . be alone, in my room, at the Mystic, Hilton, that night . . . or not! I was just happy, that, the four of us, myself, Anthony, his Mum, JoAnn, my new friend and her husband, David, "Sarge," would be together.

Perhaps, in time, more would come from our togetherness. Mandel was funny and JoAnn and I got to, meet and greet him, that night. She and I, sat, in the control booth, at center stage, in the middle, of the Fox Theatre We had, the best 2 seats, in the house, thanks to, a friend of Sarge, while, at the show, Anthony and Sarge, gambled and hung out.

The four of us . . . got together, again and the men, gambled, until just past, 1 a.m. I was glad, when Anthony followed us, me, in Sarge's SUV, with Sarge and JoAnn, to the Mystic, Hilton. We all, said, our goodnights and Anthony, came, to my room. We smoked, a small marijuana cigarette and I, went into the shower. I didn't know, if he would be there, when I came out.

I had bought, a lingerie set, at, Fredrick's, of Hollywood, in the event, he did, come to, my room and would, remain. Now, as soon as

I did, come out, of the shower, I laid, on the bed and Anthony, was still there . . . he got into the shower. While I laid, in the bed, quietly reminiscing, about our two prior, lovemaking encounters, yet, not knowing . . . if he, would give me . . . another, "chip!" since, it was still, just . . . February, in fact, Valentine's Weekend . . . or just, sleep with me, in, my room and or leave.

I waited, anxiously, patiently, to see, what he would do. He DID, come into me, again, as a man and gave, himself to me, fully and completely and without, reservation. His essence lulled me, into a deep, restful, blissful, sleep. Oh! . . . At about 5 a.m., I woke up, to use the ladies room. Anthony was sitting . . . at the small, table, smoking a cigarette! The ashtray was full, of cigarette butts! What seemed . . . a whole pack!

He was, in his clothes and seemed, very restless . . . and even . . . annoyed! "What's wrong, Anthony?!?" I asked. "I haven't slept, all night, Cynthia, I've been sitting here, smoking cigarettes. I CAN'T sleep!" he said, sternly. "Please . . . come lie down and try to get some sleep!?!" I said. "No, I have to go; I have to go . . . right now! . . . Goodbye, Cynthia!"

With that, he got up, put on, his coat and left. When 9 a.m. came, JoAnn called. I told her, about Anthony. I was disappointed, he wasn't, going to join us, for breakfast . . . he just . . . took off! No real . . . reason . . . why!?! JoAnn, tried to comfort me, at breakfast, saying, she and Anthony, both suffer, insomnia.

Well, I pretended, to understand, yet, I was DEEPLY HURT, and disillusioned . . . It wasn't March? I didn't ask, for a chip? . . . He gave himself, without ANY, request and so . . . SOON AGAIN!?! Now, was he mad at me, himself, or was he truly repulsed . . . to be in bed . . . with me?!? after all . . . I did not know, why he had sex, with me, in the Hilton . . . all I knew, was he didn't want, to sleep the night, with me, or eat breakfast with me, or . . . well . . . I was totally, confused and devastated.

I tried, not to call him, or see him, for a few days. He didn't call me, either. The leaky roof was still not, under control, we were going nowhere, fast. So that next, Wednesday night, I was very depressed, that so many days, had passed and no contact, with Anthony. Diane said, "Let's go out drinking tonight! And I said, "Okay! I need a good drunk!

We went, to the Hideaway Bar, in Colchester, Connecticut. We drank, all night and had girl talk, about the husbands and men, in general. About midnight, a nice looking man, came, by my right side. I could tell, he was attracted, to me. Drunk, as we both were, we hit it off. Ha! Ha! Ha! He drove, my white Benz and we took, Diane, to her car, at the exit 23, commuter lot.

His name, was Zachary and he was, a navy brat, my same age, unmarried, with a two year old, son, who was at, his Mums for, the night and Zachary, told me we could, "Stay out, all night!" I was, drunk and certainly game, after all . . . Anthony, had dumped me, in the Hilton, days earlier and I, hadn't heard, nor did I know, if I would . . . hear from him?!?

Zachary, was funny, smart, sexy, my same age and listened, to me cry, over Anthony. He asked me to, drive him, home and invited me, in, for a nightcap. Well . . . his nightcap, turned into, a sexcapade, which lasted, until, sunrise! He slayed me! I didn't love, or want him, yet, the physical chemistry, took both of us, by storm. He had a voracious, sexual appetite, which he fulfilled, several times, in succession, all night long. Huh! I, was to do, nothing, he insisted, to do everything I was treated, to a sexual encounter, strictly physical, not romantic . . . BAR NONE!

I thought, those types of things, only happened, in a Penthouse Forum . . . now, I had lived it! Or . . . had I. I was dying, inside, for . . . Anthony.

Cynthia.

Chapter 33

The very next afternoon, Anthony, finally called. He was strictly, business as if; we never, even . . . touched! I was so hurt, yet took, his crumbs and agreed, to meet him, regarding only, our business partnership. Zachary, had said, he wanted to see me, again and Anthony, pretended, we never, ever, touched! What, was I, to do?!?

I was, so lonely, for only, Anthony's, love and physicality . . . for the, rest of my life! Yet, now, he seemed, more distant, than ever! We did some stops, at the, construction site and furniture shopping and . . . all the while . . . it was all, strictly business. Inside, I was, dying and hurt, yet longing, in burning desire, consuming my soul, for Anthony, to love me, need me, want me, as I did . . . him!

That evening, before I went home, I told him off!!! for using me, for sex, at the Hilton. I told him, he was a, hypocrite, a lousy, lover and quote, "I've had better, since you, you suck, as a lover!" unquote. With that, I had sealed, my own fate . . . without, even knowing it! at that very moment! Her majesty, the baby, had to, tell off and demean, the ONLY man, she ever, TRULY loved, at FIRST SIGHT, because, he would not, love her back!

As hard as I tried, I became, more toxic, toward Anthony, with every passing day, thereafter. Soon, we had an appointment, at my lawyers, Ralph's, office, one, we both decided, was a good appointment, a co-appointment, to discuss, formation of, the corporation Star Power Productions, LLC.

The meeting went off well, until after, we left and Ralph, called my cell phone, "Come back, to the office, before you go home, I need, to talk to you!" he said. When I returned, at about 4 p.m. he kept me, until about 5:30 p.m. He told me, Anthony, was a, "Scam Artist!" and I needed to, "Have him, arrested!" He told me, to come in the, next morning and he, would go after Anthony!" for scamming me!

Now Ralph, had been, my Mothers divorce lawyer, in 1983 and we know . . . knew of each other, from that case, so . . . I did, go in the next morning, to Ralph's office. He called, the Norwich and the State of Connecticut, Police and then, insisted . . . I sign, a medical, waiver and we, go immediately, to my psychiatrist, Dr. Gene's office, to document, how Anthony . . . had scammed me?!?

Ralph and Dr. Gene, decided, that it was urgent, I go in that day! And so, that afternoon, the three of us, met and discussed, my issues, with Anthony! I told them everything! But . . . Dr. Gene, decided and Ralph, agreed, that I, would be given, 300 mg. of Lithium, 3 times a day. I was to start taking it . . . that day. I was told, to, "stay away, from Anthony!" by, both . . . my psychiatrist, Dr. Gene and lawyer, Ralph and to have, "No contact, with Anthony!"

Ralph wanted to sue, Anthony, for fraud. I spent the next 5 days, semi- comatose, in my bed, in my room, in the dark, day and night, crying, for Anthony . . . and what, I thought . . . I had lost! I was, being brainwashed, by Ralph, in person and over the phone and via . . . Lithium! Bed rest! That suing, Anthony and forgetting, about Star Power, was the thing that I needed to do.

The more, he tried to convince me, Anthony . . . was no good . . . the further, in the pit of hell, despair and depression . . . I went! On the sixth day, I was, to take the Lithium; I got out of my bed . . . instead. I crawled out and took a shower and called, Anthony. By this time, he had already been, contacted, by the Police and Ralph. I told Anthony, what my last, five days, in bed, in a Lithium, semi-coma and how I felt, about how all, the wretched things, Ralph, was trying, to convince me, about . . . him, Anthony, were destroying me.

I was dying . . . a slow-burn death—Anthony, was kind, yet stern, he agreed, to let me, visit him, just to talk . . . that evening. When all was explained, we decided, to break contact, with Ralph and get, another lawyer and move forward, with Star Power. Soon, it was March. Anthony was dating again and I was jealous . . . again!

We had a huge fight, one day, in front of, his mother, JoAnn, at his cottage, in Old Lyme. I had no right, to tell him, but I still loved, wanted needed and desired, him. He ended that romance. Soon, another, new young woman was in his life, his bed, his heart, his home!

I, had lost, all hope . . . at that point and decided, reverse psychology, would be, my only method, of coping, with yet . . . another . . . new woman, in Anthony's life! I began, to tell him, that he needed to get, "serious with, her and marry, her and that she was, quote, 'surely the one.'" Anthony's mother, JoAnn, insisted, "He won't marry, that girl!"

In my, hurt and insanely jealous desire, I continued, to distance myself, from our, business relationship and go down, a drunken party, all night long, around town mode, in the hopes, that Anthony, would want . . . to stop me! Rescue me! Love me! Once, and for all . . . he did not.

During this time, I had broken ties, with Ralph and then, rehired him, to draw, up a 14 page, operating agreement I didn't know, it was going to be, a 14 page, operating agreement . . . Ralph said, "I will, draw up an agreement" So, Ralph drew it up, this was to be, an agreement, which Anthony, would . . . as Ralph said, quote, "would have to sign, to adhere to, or else!" unquote, Ralph would say.

He insisted that if Anthony, violated, anything, in the agreement, to call, himself . . . Ralph, immediately! Anthony, reluctantly, did sign, that 14 page, operating agreement, to move forward. March and April of 2007, were very hard, indeed.

Anthony, had a new love, in his life, the studio, was almost ready, week after week, with always, some bizarre setback, it was OUT OF CONTROL! With my, drinking and going, to bars and hanging out, with my so-called, bodyguards and talent, that came in and out, of my life . . . the happier, Anthony seemed, with his new love . . . the more, miserable and lower, I sunk!

It was May, 9th, 2007. I went, to the studio, to check on, all the last minute details. Inside, were Anthony, his mum, JoAnn and his young lover, having a meeting, with an internet company, I insisted, I was not invited to! I got highly, upset and remembered, that Ralph told me, "If ONE LINE . . . of the operating agreement, was violated, to call him."

And so, I called Ralph and said, "He's got JoAnn, his mum and his, young lover, in there!" "That's it, he's 'outta there, the agreement states, no one included, by blood or marriage, put that BITCH, his mother, on the phone!" Ralph said. I went in and told her, my lawyer, wanted to talk to her. I saw, her face . . . sink, as he told her, to, "Get lost!" I drove to New London, Action Auto Insurance, because, the insurance, on Anthony and my cars, were due, that day.

I was in no mood, to pay for his SLK, for the month, so I called, his cell phone, "Anthony, you need, to get over here, to Action Auto Insurance, RIGHT NOW! You need, to pay, your $200.00, auto insurance, RIGHT NOW!" I demanded. He was, shocked and dismayed, that my lawyer, told his mother, to go away! I didn't care. I was through, caring for someone, who could, hurt me intentionally or, so I thought.

I felt, the victim, of his callous, loveless ness and blatant, parade, of young lovers, before my, sight and through, our business, endeavor and I, the GREAT, I . . . had, had enough! No more, JoAnn, no more, lover, in MY STUDIO! I reasoned, to myself. Of course, Ralph called me over and over, that day and came down, hard on Anthony, again and in his, speeches to me, at the office, on my way home.

When I did get there, during his speeches . . . right before . . . Ralph, hugged me and consoled me and promised me, that he, would come, to my rescue! And so, Ralph, started calling, all the shots! He told me, to have, the locks changed, on the studio building, the next day! And that, this time, Anthony, would be sued, for fraud, because, he was a, "scam artist," and would, "end up, in jail!"

Cynthia.

Chapter 34

So there I was, now in the throws, of a twisted, sexual, hell, with Ralph . . . missing . . . and still, deeply in love, with Anthony. Miserable, still, at home, in my marriage and now, having to face, running a recording studio, which I knew, NOTHING ABOUT, at all . . . by myself?!? I was petrified, yet couldn't move, my own chess piece, of life, toward or backward, as Ralph, had total control, of my behaviors, my mindset!

I needed someone, to help me, because, Anthony was gone, forced out, by Ralph and Ralph, absolutely, forbid me, to contact Anthony, not to mention, that Ralph, also, had me get the FBI, involved, due to the cache, of elephant tusks, Anthony, was trying to sell. My life was a total mess, my person, a total, wreck and now, I had to try and function!

Then, it came to me! Ah! I remembered . . . One fine afternoon, in late March, of 2007, when Anthony and I, had gone, to the Crystal Mall, in Waterford, Connecticut, to buy clove incense. There is a small, narrow, shop, which sells, various items, including crystals, jewelry, wizards, games, knives, swords and the like. It is, what I'd consider, reminiscent, of a 1970's, head shop.

Well, anyhow, we walked in and Anthony was, picking the incense. I saw two, young black men, in the right hand aisle. Anthony took the left aisle, to go and pay. I noticed, the two young men, showing a third young man, a knife. Instantly, I decided, to talk, to the three, young men. I said, "Excuse me, do you guys, want to know, how to win, a knife fight?!?"

The tallest most built young man, handling the knife, said, "Yeah . . . with my gun!" "No," I said, "Now, I'll tell you . . . hopefully, you strike, the first blow, if not, you dive for, the feet and take, the knife and cut . . . one . . . better yet, both, of your opponents, Achilles tendons, they're all DONE! They're not going, ANYWHERE!"

"For real?" the young man said. His friend answered, "Yeah! I heard something about that!" The three of us, instantly, made friends. I told them, I owned, a recording studio, soon to open, in Groton, on Poquonnock Road and introduced them to my partner, Anthony. The tall man, was named Meik, his friend, was Ray. We exchanged phone numbers, on the spot. That was not unusual, because, Anthony and I had scouted talent, every time; we went out, in public.

Well, later on, that particular day, in March, I was on the way, to see Asher, whom, I had been seeing and studying Kabbalah, Judaism with, since he first, read my palm, the year before! Who, was, on the last turn, toward the Rabbi, Asher's, apartment? But Meik! He was, at a buddy's house, on the sidewalk, I was so happy . . . to see him again! Since, we had only met, about three hours, before . . . in the knife store!

I pulled over and hollered, "Meik, its Cynthia! How cool! It is . . . we meet AGAIN . . . and on the, SAME DAY! With that, I leapt, out of, my Benz and we gave each other, a huge hug! I could tell, we would become, TRUE FRIENDS! And . . . we did. We had kept, in touch and it was, Meik, I would call, to help me, in my studio, dilemma!

Because, on the first day, we met, he assured me, that we were, quote, "Meant to meet, become, friends and he assured me . . . he HAD MY BACK!" unquote.

As fate, would have it, Meik knew, about the studio business, a bit, because, he, was involved, briefly, once before, with a cousin, but . . . it had ended. I called Meik and told him, everything, I was facing. He piled, his two, small children and wife, in the car and came immediately, to meet me, at the studio!

I, started crying, when they first arrived . . . I was, so scared and didn't know, how . . . I could, go on?!? With everything, I had gone through, I broke down, totally and he and his wife, tried, to console me, he said "C, I told you, the day we met, I got your back! I, will help you, finish and open, this studio! You have, my WORD! You will OPEN, we will MAKE MUSIC, we will give it, ALL WE HAVE and if, WE GO DOWN, WE GO DOWN . . . TOGETHER!

You are my Godmother, C, now so . . . quit crying . . . Meik and the FAMILY, are HERE NOW! We, are your FAMILY now, my wife and my kids, are your, FAMILY and now, my ENTIRE FAMILY . . . is YOUR FAMILY NOW and WE

WON'T ABANDON YOU, we will, LOVE YOU and your husband . . . you will NEVER be LONELY AGAIN, C!"

EVERYTHING, Meik told me, came completely true. That night, he called his Uncle, in to decide, just what, needed to be done, to finish up and get us, a certificate of occupancy. Also, that night, several, of his friends, arrived and relatives, who had eventually, also, become, my new GODCHILDREN! And also, call me, "Ma!"

Each new day, brought new, young people, good people, positive people and then . . . the artists, started arriving! Meik, made it all happen. He found the engineer, he found the artists, he knew the talent, we were BUSY, EVERY DAY, from the end of May, until the end of July, making music, good music, all of us, pro bono, sweat equity, on volunteer basis, hoping and working, toward our first . . . hit! Which, would hopefully, launch us into the market.

We did all, we could, we had a huge ad campaign on, the radio and Alex, was financially, backing everything. We all worked, so hard and then, one hot day, July 31, 2007 to be exact, it all had to stop! Alex was, out of money and we, at the studio, were out of business. As bittersweet, as it was, to throw in, the towel and close the studio, I had, GAINED EVERYTHING! I would ever need, again, in my life.

I got my life back, I got my self esteem back, I got my dignity, back and ALL . . . THANKS, TO MEIK and the family, coming to my rescue. From the day, he and his family and friends, came into my life, the quality, of my life, improved! He and they, showed me, TRUE BROTHERLY, MOTHERLY, as this case may be . . . LOVE!

Meik, showed me, how to LIVE AGAIN! Not, placing my, personal happiness, or well being, onto whether, I had a man . . . be it, Anthony, Alex, or other, to love me. He and the family showed me, the greater value, of brotherly love, each one of us should have! And show, one another, on this earthly journey . . . through, the human condition. From day one, I learned, to live, a more, dignified lifestyle again!

I didn't need, to go out, partying to nightclubs and casinos, anymore and get, intoxicated into oblivion . . . or worse! And, I didn't need, sexual encounters, with emptiness and self loathing, anymore! We worked hard, yet . . . we played hard . . . we had some, nice times, at the studio, good, clean, fun! Pizza parties, coffee and doughnuts, a graduation party, for Meik's wife, Hiquikah, from nursing school and we, offed and had, a huge picnic, at Mohegan Park and especially, in July, for his Mum, Vanessa's 43rd Birthday!

Every day, we were together, my life got, better and better and I had, begun to write . . . this work . . . and I learned, how to be happy, again and I felt, loved, for the first time, in many years. My own, remaining, blood relatives and myself, are not, on the same wavelength. We're just too different, in our, lifestyles and emotions and that, is all okay . . . live and let live!

The old saying, "You can choose, your friends, but you can't, choose your relatives!" is so, TRUE! I do not, choose to associate, with my relatives, currently and they, feel the same way, about me. The relationships, were very . . . Ah . . . as one would say, "One sided," in the latter years, they, needed and wanting, something that I could do, for them, financially, or emotionally, with little or no, reciprocation. I felt, used and unloved, by them, by my remaining, blood kin . . . and I love them . . . to this day!

I was, more compatible, with all the elders and they had all passed away! I had, accepted it, or so I thought and I'm very sure, the lack of love, from them, my husband and then, the apple of my eye, Anthony, nearly, broke my spirit . . . for good! It was Meik, and all the people, he brought, into my life, that SAVED ME!!! From my own, pit of despair and feeling, there wasn't much, to live for anymore!

EVERYTHING CHANGED, for the better, the positive; I was living in harmony, with my spiritual essence, again, FINALLY! Meik, gave me the strength, to stop Ralph, from using me, for sex, stop drinking outside of at home, give up pot and basically, straighten up and fly right!

It was, during the time with Meik, at the studio, that I began, to understand, what PURPOSE, everything, I was going through, or had gone through, from a baby, had brought me to. My TRUE PURPOSE, the one my FATHER, had dubbed me with.

As I began, to think, clearly and rationally, again, I could see too, that my, Roman Catholic persona, my student of Kabbalah, persona and my birthright persona, were coming into, total alignment. The triangulation, of the three elements, were, cathartic and had given me, the clarity, to understand all, my Father had, taught me and told me, prophesied to me, was my life's, purpose and my destiny, as the Golden Child, female . . . the Luna Leo Theo Sophia, as predicted, by the, Countess of Caithness, Scotland, in the year, 1876, perhaps, or '75.

When last, I saw my Father, in December of 2004, he filled me in, on the true purpose of, my life and times and described, what my future, would hold, if I overcame . . . the last test . . . of the Creator. And so, I did overcome the last test.

Before, I can reveal the truth, to you, who reads, or hears this and to, the entire world, for that matter . . . NOW IS THE TIME, the time is, at hand and the truth, is the Secret of the Red String, which I am finally, strong enough and balanced, enough . . . to share, in love . . . with you.

Cynthia.

Chapter 35

The TRUTH . . . The moment of truth, the truth, of the title, of this book, in its entirety, for now . . .

The secret of the red string, begins in the 12th generation, after Noah, entered the ark. Noah, had many children, among them, a son named Bith, which is not mentioned, in the Torah, or, Pentateuch and another, named Japhet, who is mentioned. Bith, had a daughter, named Cessair . . . and Japhet, who is mentioned, in the Torah, had a son, named Magog.

Well, this female grandchild, of Noah, Cessair, upon seeing her Grandfather, Noah, building the ark, decided to build, an IDOL! Now, Cessair built, the idol, and the idol, would speak, to her and told her, "Build her own ship! Forget about the ark! to escape, the coming Deluge!" Cessair, did it and she and her husband Fintan and all, their followers, set sail, for 7 years, to find a place, where the idol, told them, to escape the coming, Deluge.

They all landed, on Donemark, Bounty Bay, in 'em, County Cork, in what is now called . . . IRELAND! Forty days, before the flood! Cessair's husband, Fintan, became afraid, of the coming, Deluge and left, Cessair, on a small raft, he built, himself, soon after landing. Then, Cessair, died six days, after he left, of a broken heart, six days, before the flood.

Everyone that followed, Cessair and Fintan, on the idol ship, built . . . DIED . . . in the flood. Now, Fintan, himself, while on the raft, he had built and fell, into the sea. He was said, to have come back, again . . . as a man, who spoke to Starn.

Now, Starn, was the brother, of a sixth generation, descendant of Noah, from the fruit of, Japhet and Magog. Starn, himself, remembered his direct lineage to Noah . . . and his brother Partholon and the story, of the flood, which Starn, handed down, to his descendants, including, Agnoman of Scythia and also, their heritage, as Neolithic farmers.

These things are TRUE. I tell you! Agnoman of Scythia, had a son, named . . . Nemed, which . . . Meant . . . "Holy privileged son!" Nemed, begat Artur, who died, Iarbonel, father of Semul, Annind, who had no, sons and Fergus the Red Side, eldest, who had no sons. And then, of course, as spoken before, there was Starn, the younger, who begat Beoan.

Nemed, was the, "Keeper," of the secret of the red string, his father, Agnoman of Scythia, told him . . . always . . . to have the YOUNGEST, son rule FIRST . . . not, the eldest and then, the ELDEST, in the event of, death and then the NEXT, youngest and the next, eldest and so on.. In that, sequential order, unless or until, a decision, had to be made, that one was, NOT WORTHY . . . of the secret of the red string OR, if the secret . . . would, DIE and be LOST, FOREVER!

The ruler, at that time, who could see, that the secret, could possibly die and be LAST FOREVER . . . LOST . . . would HAVE TO ACQUIESCE . . . to

SAVE THE SECRET OF THE RED STRING! And so, as time, went on, this had to be DONE UNTIL THE LAST . . . even until, I AM speaking, to you today! As not, to let the secret die, until the time, The GOD OF NOAH, the feminine deity, would, come to the earth, and reveal, the secret, just BEFORE the next DESTRUCTION, of the EARTH, not by flood, but . . . BY FIRE!!!

The secret, was to be preserved, at all costs, down through time, until, the EXACT TIME, the CREATOR, the GOD OF NOAH, had instructed his son, JAPHET, to hand down, to the twelfth, generation and that the name, would have to be changed, to PROTECT, the IDENTITY, of feminine deity, as DIRECT DESCENDANT OF NOAH, her first FATHERLY ANCESTOR, DOWN, THROUGH TIME!

When Starn the younger died, he gave the secret, to his only son, Beoan, who gave it, to his only son, Erglan. Erglan, had five sons, which, were the twelfth, generation, of Noah. Slaine, was the youngest. He became, the FIRST HIGH KING, OF IRELAND!

And just as instructed, the eldest . . . Rudraige, then ruled, as second High King, of Ireland, upon Slaine's death. When Rudraige died, the twins . . . Gann and Genann, ruled together. When the last one died . . . the middle son, of all five, birth survivors, Sengann, ruled.

They ALL KNEW, the secret of the, red string and Sengann, DECREED, that the FOUNDATION of the NAME be CHANGED, from Gann . . . to GUNN! To protect, the identity, of the feminine deity, down through TIME! DIANA, Princess, of Wales . . . Diana Spencer-Windsor, was MURDERED, because she was thought . . . to be . . . the Lunar deity, who would . . . CHANGE THE WORLD!!! And I tell you, as sure as I am, sitting here today . . . Henri Paul, was commissioned, to be, the SUICIDE ASSASIN, by QUEEN ELIZABETH the second, HERSELF!!!

She, is NOT, THE TRUE MONARCH, OF CELTS, I, CYNTHIA ANNE MARIE GUNN, AM!!!

Now, it would not be prudent, wise or productive, for me to go further . . . AT THIS MOMENT!!! Suffice, to say, that THE VATICAN, Queen Elizabeth the second, the FREEMASONS, the KNIGHTS TEMPLAR . . . and . . . the KABBALAH RABBIS, who DAILY, WAIL and MOURN and WEEP, at the WESTERN WALL in JERUSALEM, KNOW EXACTLY . . . WHO I AM!!!

I make this proclamation, as a MATTER OF FACT, because MY ANCESTOR, MARY QUEEN OF SCOTS, had to adhere, to the secret, of the red string and ACQUIESCE, to Queen Elizabeth the first, daughter of Henry and Anne Boleyn, herself, as not to be, shed . . . any more, Scottish blood and to, protect the identity, of the TRUE MONARCHY, TRUE MONARCHY, down THROUGH TIME, until NOW!!!

My Father, William Thomas Phillip Gunn, was the TRUE KING, OF SCOTLAND and TIME, TRUE, to FORM, and to MY IDENTITY, he passed, me LINEAGE and THESE TRUTHS, down to me. The GUNNS were HERE, IN AMERICA, BEFORE CHRISTOPHER COLUMBUS, by approximately,

ONE HUNDRED YEARS!!! The GUNNS, found AMERICA, that is how, I AM able, TO CLAIM, QUEEN OF AMERICA . . . the PROOF, is CARVED,

on a CLIFF, in a NEW ENGLAND STATE and I, will be REVEALING and PROVING, more in depth . . . SHORTLY, regarding myself, my GOD GIVEN, ABILITIES and my . . . MISSION.

My ancient, weathered and modern, TARTANS . . . BEAR, THE RED STRING!!! The MASONS, BEAR THE GUNN, MONOGRAM . . .

My next WORK, MY LOVES, will be the BLUEPRINT, OF ETERNAL LIFE . . . and I, GUARANTEE IT!!! So, PLEASE, TAKE HEART, BE PATIENT and LEARN . . . ACCEPT . . .

The Creator hasn't, given up, on us, just YET!!!

Love, Cynthia

Chapter 36

"Ode to Mother . . ." On behalf, of my Mother, Celene, thank you all, for being here today. For those of you, who have a, twenty-four-hour book, when you have a quiet moment, I'd like to recommend, reading Mums first, thought for the day, October 22nd, in the year, 1975. Today's, thought for the day, IS:

We cannot, get along, without prayer and meditation. On awakening, let us think, about the twenty-four-hours . . . ahead! We consider, our plans for the day . . . before we begin, we ask GOD the CREATOR, to direct our thinking. Our thought lives, will be placed, on a MUCH HIGHER PLAIN . . . when we start, the day, with prayer and meditation. We conclude, this period of meditation, with a prayer, that we will be shown, throughout the day, what our NEXT STEP IS TO BE!!!

The basis, of all of our prayers, IS . . . THY WILL BE DONE!!! In me and through me TODAY!!! Am I, sincere, in my DESIRE, TO DO, THE CREATOR, GOD'S WILL TODAY?

Breathe in, the inspiration; of GOODNESS and TRUTH . . . it is THE SPIRIT, of HONESTY, PURITY, UNSELFISHNESS and LOVE!!! It is READILY AVAILABLE . . . IF we are WILLING, to ACCEPT IT, WHOLEHEARTEDLY.

GOD, the CREATOR, has GIVEN us, MANY THINGS, His SPIRIT and the POWER . . . OF CHOICE!!! Are the, TWO GREATEST . . . to ACCEPT . . . or

not, as we WILL. We have the GIFT of FREE WILL!!!

When, we choose the path of selfishness . . . and greed . . . and pride . . . we are, refusing to ACCEPT, GOD THE CREATORS SPIRIT. When, we choose the path of . . . LOVE and SERVICE, we accept, God the Creators, spirit and it FLOWS INTO US and . . . MAKES ALL THINGS . . . NEW!!!

I pray, that I may CHOOSE the RIGHT WAY . . . I pray . . . that I may TRY to FOLLOW IT, TO . . . THE END!!! AMEN.

Love, Cynthia . . .

www.ingramcontent.com/pod-product-compliance
Lightning Source LLC
Chambersburg PA
CBHW030328100526
44592CB00010B/609